Marian C

C000140438

STOPPING SCHOOL VIOLENCE

One Teacher's Silent Scream

Dedicated to Shannon Wright, an extraordinary teacher.

SILVERSMITH
PRESS

Published by Silversmith Press–Houston, Texas
www.silversmithpress.com

Copyright © 2024 Marian Carlino

All rights reserved.

This book, or parts thereof, may not be reproduced in any form or by any means without written permission from the publisher, except for brief passages for purposes of reviews.

The views and opinions expressed herein belong to the author and do not necessarily represent those of the publisher.

ISBN 978-1-961093-34-8 (Softcover Book)
ISBN 978-1-961093-35-5 (eBook)

CONTENTS

v

CONTENTS

CHAPTER 1

A SOBERING REALITY

My day started as any ordinary day. The school bell rang. I stood in front of the children as they settled in their seats. We were just beginning the opening exercises when the fire alarm rang, complete with strobe lights and Man from U.N.C.L.E sirens. We gathered in line to exit quickly. Confused by the new sounds and visual effects, I forgot my attendance record but could not go back to get it. We walked in straight lines to the playground, leaving the building for the first fire drill in the new school. When it concluded, we returned to the sanctuary of the classroom.

1,130 miles away, in another school, the fire bell rang. Children and adults walked quietly out to the school yard. Everyone knew the drill. But this one would be different. Two middle school students lured their unsuspecting classmates and teachers outside. Armed with guns, they opened fire, and waged war. By the end of the rampage, four female students and one teacher were dead. An extraordinary day in Jonesboro, Arkansas, changed the trajectory of lives, including mine. The heroic woman, who saved the life of one student, did not know she'd saved mine.

On March 24, I left work to pick up my two school-aged children. Already tense from the day, I heard the heart wrenching news. While parking, I read the large sign asking for prayers for the school in Jonesboro. Reality, in full view, erased my complacency.

At the after-school program, I greeted my children and the staff, and then asked for paper and a pencil to jot a note of thanks to whomever put the words on the sign. I do not remember what I wrote, I was so overwrought. Crying, I handed the paper to the staff member as I signed my kids out for the day. The sign must have hit a nerve with the administration because it came down before the next morning.

For us, March 24, 1998, started with the fire department testing the equipment and setting off an unexpected drill with siren alarms and strobe lights new to the staff and students. Opening exercises stopped abruptly. We returned to the room, resumed our schedule with sharing time, a meaningful part of the day. Given the opportunity to share, one boy did tell us about his previous afternoon. Listening to what this child said, another student rose to speak. He expressed significant anger at the boy, directing all his comments to him, not to the class. He said he had phoned to make plans the previous day to speak but did not receive a return call and expressed disappointment and anger at the perceived change of plan.

It was an unfortunate mistake. I had put an assignment on the second boy's desk thinking it belonged to him. There were initials on the paper, but another child had the same initials, so I had handed the paper to the wrong student. He argued with me about it. I apologized, but he could not be placated, and his anger just kept rising. Changes and interruptions are hard on some children.

After our lunch, we divided into small groups. Several boys, including the two from the morning conversation, had organized to write a story. The two started arguing about statistics. The angry boy would not stop. The argument became so loud, I sent them to their seats and instructed them to get something else to do. One took out his math book and got to work, but the angry student continued to argue across the room. I gave warnings but they went unheeded. I told him if he did not get to work, I would call the Principal. He continued his inappropriate behavior until I picked up the room telephone. He made a motion to sit down, but his eyes and face warned me the episode was not over. It warranted time out. I phoned the office to tell the secretary that I was sending this child to the Principal. Then I phoned the learning resource teacher so she could escort him.

Within a few minutes of being sent, the child and the Principal came back to the class. When they entered the room, she came over towards me, interrupting my teaching and told me that I could not keep him out of gym. She specified that it was against his IEP. This Individualized Education Plan is a program to ensure that a child with an identified disability who is attending school receives specialized instruction. I told her that I disagreed, and that the child would be back to her office. I did not whisper it. She stormed out of the room.

The child went to gym and so did the Principal. She made several trips back and forth to the gymnasium to keep an eye on him. She informed me he had done very well. He did maintain his composure, typical behavior after an outburst, intervention, and visible monitoring.

While I stood in the office, the Principal came in and asked me if I had a moment. I looked at the clock. It was 3:30 p.m., well past time that I could have left for the day, but I said, "Yes." As we stepped into the office, she proceeded to tell me that she was writing me up as being unprofessional for disagreeing with her, with no mention of the child's inappropriate behavior. I did tell her that if she had to, she should go ahead, but I would rebut anything, especially if placed in my file. That statement ushered in a challenge to her.

On March 25, still reeling from news of the shooting at Jonesboro, we had a half day. A workshop scheduled for the afternoon meant early dismissal at 12:45 pm. I took this as an opportunity to meet with the school psychologist to discuss the deteriorating behaviors of this student and the Principal's involvement the previous day. The psychologist reminded me that the IEP classified child had rights that the others did not have. Then I checked my mailbox at about 1:00 p.m. and saw a notice from the Principal headed "Notice of Improvement Needed." Sometimes typo errors tell a story. March 24 was a Tuesday. The Principal noted our encounter as occurring on Tuesday, March 23. The date was not the only thing she got wrong.

Notice of Improvement Needed

Mrs. Carlino, according to our teacher appraisal criteria, staff is to show sensitivity to students at all times. In addition, teachers are to choose proper techniques when working with our students. After our encounter on Tuesday, March 23, I am noticing you that I expect improvement on your part in both areas. When my office staff told me that a student of yours would be coming to my office for cooling-off, I responded immediately. I took care of the situation. The student mentioned that as a result of arguing on and off that day, he was asked to leave the room. He also mentioned he was going to lose his physical education period with his classmates. I consulted your schedule to see that there was a scheduled class in physical education, not recess. I am sure you're aware that, as a technique, it is inappropriate for a student to be kept from any course which is offered to the students, and it is inappropriate for a student to be kept from any course as punishment. I told the child that, now that he was calm and had vented about a variety of issues, and he really needed to, I had decided that at my level, the child was ready to return to class and he was just in time for the 12:35 p.m. physical education class.

The notice went on:

When I asked you if physical education was scheduled for 12:35 p.m., you said that he couldn't take physical education. I quietly said to you that you can't keep a child from a class. I wouldn't have returned him if I hadn't seen that he was calm and communicating in a safe manner, and he assured me that he knew what behavior was appropriate for his classroom. In my opinion, he was ready to return to the group.

As I left the room you said in front of the other children, across the room something like, "Fine, but he'll be right back to you." The statement, on your part, was not only unprofessional, but also unkind. In addition, as the Principal of the school I would hope that, in the future, if you disagree with me, you could save your comments for a time when the children were not in the room.

Yes, you've been working well with this child addressing his many needs, but for a teacher to predict failure on the part of a student in front of the other students is unacceptable. According to law, as you know, this is a classified student, whose classification includes a label of emotionally disturbed. We must be careful to ascertain if his actions are result of his handicapping condition. If so, he cannot be excluded from activities or suspended from school. It is very appropriate to give him a cooling-off period when needed, so he can pull himself together. However, once he is calm and ready to return, a teacher cannot exclude him from the program. The child's handicapping condition is that of attention deficit disorder with oppositional defiant components. His behavior must continue to be handled by you as the school psychologist has directed.

Do not construe any of this to mean that I demand we keep a child in class when he or she is unable to control his or her outbursts. Again, the cooling down period works well for him. Please help the other children in the class to see that you have hope for him and not that you predict future failure. I look forward to improvement in this area.
 Signed, the Pipa (the Principal)

And with that notice served on me, I took a step forward in the hope of a brighter future, and on a road less traveled. When starting, direction is necessary. Plan a party, a trip, an educational choice, or a career change, do we go blindly? Most likely, no: we seek guides. Leaps of faith are not led by those who cannot see.
 A storm was brewing; there were changes on the horizon. I had to get there "the best way I knew how." I had some experience in that. In 1989, I had also had a big problem while planning a trip. I had a toddler and five weeks post C-section after giving birth to my son. How was I to make the journey? I asked the person closest to me. The response, "Get there the best way you know how." The words seemed harsh and selfish; however, they became part of my way of journeying. I got to my destination, entrusting my five-week-old son to my mother-in-law and my toddler and me to the hands of my brother-in-law and sister. The road was wet, but everyone inside the car, even the toddler, remained dry.

CHAPTER 1

Prayer is talking and listening to God. He listens and equips us for the journey. It is not easy, but God engages us to picture the future.

Myth: There is no God.

THE SCREAM

Multiple shootings in schools made national headlines during the 1996-98 years, the main difference being the locations. The struggle was real, but the reality only lasted until the news dropped the story. No one wanted to admit the possibilities of the same thing happening in their school or community.

The Principal's notice of improvement to me proved to be quite severe, formal and different than the other informal threats that I had received in writing or in chats that year. Contradictions are often the case in difficult situations and the Principal's letter was full of them. But I knew my intuitions were correct. The child had repeatedly demonstrated the tendency to take his anger out on others. He had to have his way. More venting was not the answer: accepting accountability for behaviors was. While we often deal with symptomatic behaviors that have underlying causes, enabling this child to continue to act out was detrimental to us all. The Principal's statements directly opposed past practices with this child's IEP. While the statutes on maintaining safety were clear in 1998, unfortunately, those who work individually with children often do not see the other students' rights.

After I received the letter, I spoke with the grievance chairs who advised me to speak with our local association President. Earlier in the year when I met with them over similar issues; they had suggested that I meet with the Principal to discuss problems but warned me "Do not let her know she is getting to you." That was not easy. "Betty Barracuda," a CST Director when I started teaching, told me to be a bit more deceptive. "Your thoughts are written all over your face," she said with an intent to offend. Pipa, the Principal, operated on the same continuum. With the chain of command, teachers are often at a disadvantage because power and control can interfere with our desire to stop escalating behaviors. The perpetrators don't always carry a gun; some carry the keys to the main office.

Leaving the grievance chair meeting, I ran into another teacher. She and I did voluntary work together and were members of the same parish. She saw my face and knew there were problems. I told her I was taking the situation to a greater authority. She asked if I meant God. I did, but I also meant the Superintendent. God listens, but the Superintendent lived in the earthly chain of command.

I addressed the notice in a rebuttal and workshop request to the Principal, the Child Study Team, and the Superintendent. I copied it to the President of our local association and to the teachers who worked with me. We did not have to reinvent safety because the existing statutes and policies made clear the methods of maintaining control.

I sensed an urgent situation since we'd heard disturbing comments at a parents' meeting with the learning resource room teacher (LRC) and a member of the Child Study Team (CST). Nevertheless, with recent conversations concerning the history of violent outbursts and the access to guns, I felt it was timely to act. My husband doubted I should say anything, but I told him I had no choice because I could not allow a shooting. In our discussion I said if something happened, he, my husband, would have had to go public. That solution did not sit well. Why place responsibility on him? At the same time, aggressive behaviors in schools were escalating. Children do act in the ways they learn from adults.

After reading the notice and seeking professional opinion from association members, I went to a Lenten church service seeking spiritual guidance regarding this matter. The recommendations from both the association members and the Gospel message were similar. Both recommendations were to remain positive, and the Gospel message added forgiveness, giving and receiving it. With both messages in mind, I submitted this rebuttal.

Response to Notice of Improvement by the Principal dated 3/24/1998

It is with great sadness that I find myself at odds once again with the Principal regarding the interpretation of my sensitivity to students and my techniques for working with our students. I know that the Principal and I share the same values about the quality of teaching and respect for children. We have often had discussions in which opinions are mutually shared. As the Principal noted in her letter of improvement, I've been working well with this child, addressing his many needs. The Gospel message is about forgiveness. Therefore, I'm seeking the Principal's forgiveness of my inappropriate response to her. I felt that the child would soon be back to your office if he did not have enough cooling-off time. Stating it within the classroom setting was my mistake. Although poorly stated, it came after a day of stress and tension in the classroom because of the child's inappropriate outbursts to other children.

Documentation shows that sending this child to physical education class without sufficient time out could be dangerous to the safety of the other children. As the Principal is aware, my responsibility is to all the children assigned to my charge, not just the one child in question. I thank God that I saw the need for this child to have time out before allowing him to attend the PE class. The child was given the opportunity to vent his feelings about various issues in the safety of a one-to-one setting. Fortunately, the Principal deemed only a short time out was necessary.

The Gospel message also stated that to receive forgiveness, one must be willing to give it. Therefore, I do offer forgiveness to the Principal for the harsh words, innuendos, false statements, and the fact that she took the word of a child exhibiting oppositional defiant behavior over the recommendation of a professional member of her staff. I realize that the Principal also has experienced stress and tension working to help this child during the last three years.

As requested, I do not construe that she demands that a child exhibiting uncontrollable outbursts be kept in class. I realize, as does the Child Study Team, that this child needs to be separated

9

for his safety as well as the safety of the other children. The legal IEP document for this child does not exempt him from the district's behavior policy.

Every experience in life is for growing and learning. The child is learning through his experiences, and so am I, as his classroom teacher. Because of this latest experience, I have learned that I'm not doing enough for this child. As recommended by the Principal, I will certainly increase my efforts to show this child that I have hope for his future. I will exhibit a more visible and vocal roll as an advocate for this child's future. I will continue to demonstrate my sincere desire to improve his chances for a better future by showing the children in my class acceptance of his positive and appropriate behavior. I will also continue to demonstrate that some behaviors are neither appropriate, nor acceptable in a social setting. I will also continue to instruct this child that some behaviors are clearly unsafe for him.

In addition, under a separate letter, I will document that I feel this child needs one-to-one intervention by the school psychologist, so he has more opportunity to discuss what is bothering him. I look forward to an improved working relationship with the Principal because of this letter. In light of the recent violent outbursts this country has witnessed involving school age children killing other school age children, we must be aware that we may be seeking forgiveness of another sort if we do not work together as a team to brighten this child's future.

Respectfully submitted [Marian R. Carlino]

In my role, I did take that roll. The typo mistakes tell a story.

March 25, 1998, Request for Staff Meeting or Workshop

Subject: Request for further help regarding the intervention program and delivery of services to (Child's initials)

In light of the recent tragedies involving violence in our nation's schools, I feel that I would be professionally and personally wrong if I did not seek further help regarding a child in my classroom. In listening to recent news reports, discussions with professional staff members of our school, and in my daily experiences with this child, I feel that it is indeed very possible that we could be facing a similar situation as the middle school in Arkansas. Therefore, my request comes with the full understanding that I would rather be wrong and seek further intervention now, than to regret not having sought it.

I feel that all staff members, or at the very least, those dealing on a regular basis with this child, need to be in-serviced on exactly what occurs when a child diagnosed with an oppositional defiant behavior disorder is in the classroom. With this request in mind, I stated knowing that the child is not unique in receiving this diagnosis.

Documentation shows that the child's behavior has shown only slight improvement in the last three years. That is a direct result of consistent behavior management in my classroom. But unfortunately, I feel that we are only dealing with the symptoms and not resolving the problem in the long run. When the child enters less organized situations, changes in routines, arguments with parents, or feels slighted by a friend, he continues to react with the same verbal and physical violence.

(Child's initials) appears to fit the profile of some of the children whose lives have been torn apart because of their violent acts. The child is a member of a family in distress; the mother, at a recent meeting with the Child Study Team Director, Mrs. K, the LRC teacher, and me, exhibited clear frustrations. She repeated it several times when stating that her husband referred to the teachers as "bitches out to get him."

The child formed strong emotional attachments to individual classmates in kindergarten, first grade and second grade. His emotional reactions to them have often put these children in the direct line of his verbal and physical anger. He is also knowledgeable in the use of guns from his participation in Civil War Reenactments.

I am sending a copy of this request to the President of our local association, (the child's initials) kindergarten and first grade classroom teachers, as well as to the special area teachers who currently work on a daily basis with him. The more we work together as a team to improve our knowledge and approaches to working with the child, the more we can help him and other children within the school community. Respectfully submitted, Marian R. Carlino

I copied this to my coworkers: Art, Kindergarten, LRC, Physical Education, President of Local Association, first grade teachers, the Librarian, and Music teacher.

When I submitted my responses, I thought it would only take a day or two before I received their answers. The behaviors and the fact that one parent referred to the teachers as the enemy, made more escalation a real possibility. No one knows exactly when something is prevented. "Monday morning quarterbacking" and reviewing the tapes do show exactly when a violent event has not been stopped, with a classic oversight now in the 20/20 rear view mirror. I looked ahead with the knowledge of what was behind, aware that the risk for blowback was just as real.

Since the relevant staff members had received copies, the fact there was opposition was not a secret. Every teacher who worked in my room or worked directly with the child had received a copy, except for the basic skills teacher. The BSI teacher heard of it, so I explained it to her—I realized she should have received one. I did not share it with any teacher who did not have current contact, except for the eighth-grade teacher, the association President. The LRC teacher recommended that I include others who had taught him in the past, so the kindergarten teacher and the two first-grade teachers each received one. We were all well aware of the issues and needed to be apprised. The LRC teacher was genuine, so I agreed with her recommendations.

I excluded the other second grade teachers because they did not have him in their classes and two had just settled into the building. At the same time, they had a right to know because all adults share the responsibility of safety. Secrets are detrimental. Nervous about the reply, I hoped for a professional response.

It is usually one student who causes the teacher to lose sleep or lose jobs. Teachers measure their level of success against the most needy child just as a mother is only as happy as her unhappiest child. Not one of his teachers was happy or satisfied with his progress if they had been honest. Children often act out in reaction to something in their lives, and his responses at home, in school, and with his friends were troubling. Since his outbursts were not unique to school, we were dealing with symptoms and missing the causes. A child like this who had major behavioral problems as early as preschool required more than what we were offering.

In the articles and book on conduct disorders, intense therapy was indicated. He was not receiving any. The counseling was limited and then the psychologist refused to see him and deferred to the Principal for discipline. Quick fixes, happy faces and venting still do not solve anything.

I also realized that the tension between the Principal and me was strong. I had questioned her judgment, her ability to lead, and her bias when working with the child. I had also noticed she had personal connections to another child who had been exhibiting behavior problems and factored this into the equation. If we could share about one student, then we could share about all. How many children had difficulties?

On March 26, our local weekly paper ran a story about a seventh-grade student who brought a knife to school. It was brought up by one of my second grader, who at sharing time discussed that a knife had been found in a seventh-grade student's locker. I had not read the article, so I was not aware that the child had referred to our school. When I responded that serious things are happening across our country, the same child said, "No, Mrs. Carlino, it was in our school." A second grader was not reading the local paper, so parents were talking.

The timing was around the same dates as I penned my concerns. Already a child had brought in a weapon. Many parents disclosed afterwards that they were not happy with the way the administration managed the knife situation, having neither disclosed it publicly nor informed the staff. Suspending the student was the law for weapon possession on school grounds, but they would not change his locker to accommodate the safety concerns of another student's parent. So, it appeared I did not have the only problem child. Had my communication hit a nerve?

I knew that all the teachers I wrote to had similar experiences with my troubled boy. The first-grade teacher who had the boy the year before, took to the hallway and screamed to have him taken out of her class. He had his hands around a child's neck as he threw the boy into the closet. How is it that a scream in the hallway to remove a child from the class does not result in unprofessional behavior notices and reprimands? One teacher's scream is another teacher's workshop request.

My situation was far from over. On March 30, I received a memorandum with a reprimand. I was instructed to hand in all copies and to list all staff to whom I had given my letter. I gave the Principal the names not listed on the document, but I did not surrender my copies. There was no duplicity in my actions. I was trying to be cooperative while still maintaining my stand that more needed to be done.

Reluctantly, the teachers did as the principal instructed. Some shared the request with their spouses as their choice before handing in their copies. I had given it to professionals in good faith and they chose to have discussions with people worried about their safety. For this, I became a persona non grata but not before several teachers and the aide told me they agreed with me. The term, bitches, was not limited to my name, but a broad stroke of all teachers.

I still maintain that working together as a united team leads to resolutions. Stopping disruptive behaviors at elementary or middle school lessens the chance of children hurting themselves or others and from becoming destructive adults. Early intervention is recommended and should not have been met with disdain and retaliation.

The Principal's reply to my rebuttal came on March 30, 1998:

Memorandum dated 3/30/98
To: Marian Carlino
From: Principal
Subject: Reprimand

Mrs. Carlino, I acknowledge receipt of the memorandum from you dated March 25, 1998, which was addressed to Mrs. G, Mrs. F and Mrs. L with copies to 8 staff members. Mrs. Carlino, this memo was highly inappropriate and unprofessional. A request for in-service could have been made without violating the confidentiality of a classified student within our system. In addition, the memo also showed no regard for the privacy of the parent who shared personal information which she believed would stay confidential. You have violated the needless public labeling law and our policy. Further action will be taken once I have consulted with the Superintendent of Schools. You are directed to give me any copies of the memo which you have not yet distributed. In addition, I request a list of any staff or non-staff members with whom you discussed the details of this memo. Please have that list to me by 9:00 a.m. on Tuesday morning, March 31, 1998. Please sign and return. Your signature indicates receipt of this memo.

[Lines for signature of the Principal and me with cc. to the Superintendent]

The local association President told me to call the county association office for representation because my situation was beyond his area of expertise. The national associations in the 1990s were addressing violence in the journals, telling a good story, but not backing up their claims. At statewide association meetings, they constantly told us that we could not legally break up any fights. For safety reasons, we did not have to intervene directly, but we could take up the matter legally if physical intervention was needed.

Not all coworkers were sympathetic to my stand. I took them to task about the lack of action by the association with the emergency relocation. The local's secretary told others, "She is getting what she deserved"—she had no idea. As recommended, I called the county office.

I did not deliver happy face messages about the child because it would have been under false pretenses. When trying to answer to God, it means identifying the truth, which in my case meant that my classroom was not safe. Does a situation have to rise to the level of a physical fight or a shooting before action is taken?

When the handwriting on the wall spells danger, one should pay attention. Scripture states we only see partially, but God sees the plots of men and gives us timely warning. He gave me a puzzle piece. But others were afraid of the picture I was piecing together. I sensed evil in this whole situation. It was not the first time.

CHAPTER 3

ASSEMBLING
PUZZLE PIECES

Sometimes an interaction from the past factors into our days, but we do not realize the vital connection to our present—until it is well upon us. When I was the LRC teacher, I worked with a much younger basic skills instructor in a classroom which had panels dividing the room into four small modules. She also ran the after-school program and baby-sat for the Principal's children. This teacher left teaching quicker than I did—literally "here one day and gone the next." She did not stay long enough to even give anyone a chance to stand up for her or find out why she wanted to go without telling us or defending herself—if that were the case. She told me as she was leaving that she never wanted to teach again. It seems teachers can become targets of constant criticism and write ups by some principals. Disciplining other people's children can be career ending and public education has its share of refugees.

Parker Palmer, author of *The Courage to Teach*, wrote that at the microphone the private intersects with the public. When one speaks at a school board meeting, a council meeting, or in front of a crowd, one's personal beliefs become public. The dialogues and monologues can be revealing.

I have had my share of experiences with Board of Education (BOE) meetings, attending as the association advised, or whenever I could in my town. As a parent I joined the Foundation for Education.

BOE members do not want to hear from the employees and openly state it. I learned that on my first job in January 1978 when the Board delayed until well after 10:00 p.m., the formal approval of new teachers. Thinking that leaving early would put me in a bad light to the Board, I stayed until the end. I drove home that night in a blizzard which shut down most of southern N.J. for over ten days with the National Guard called into operation. That district Board always treated the teachers as adversaries. *I wonder how their attitude would factor into school safety?*

Staying through long board meetings in my local community, I heard members state they did not want to discuss certain items with anyone in the audience. However, if they could delay such considerations or debates until late into the meetings, they could speak to an empty audience with no public comment. Closed-door sessions also easily solved the problem of public disclosure.

Late in 1996-97, the BOE, who employed me, considered, and did cut several aides, with nominal savings to the budget, but hurting staff morale and community trust. Several lived in the town and had years of employment. I, together with other teachers spoke on the aides' behalf. Apprehensive of reprisals, two staff members apologized at the next meeting for speaking up but I did not.

Then again, in January 1998, the Superintendent informed all staff members that due to budget constraints the BOE had decided to eliminate special subject teachers, one librarian, one nurse, and one principal's position. The staff, extremely dismayed at the news, organized efforts to lobby to rescind the decision. We did have our rights. Tenured employees are entitled to due process and can choose to meet behind closed doors or in public. Community members and staff spoke in the open forum. The mood was as dark and gloomy as the night sky. Tension already existed between the administration and me, so I kept quiet, but I showed up anyway. I, like the teachers the year before, feared reprisals.

The administration manipulated the circumstances that evening. Eye contact is essential in discerning behavior. Hence, when people avert their gaze, it's a sure sign turmoil is brewing.

The Board rendered a decision that night to put the future of the programs and the other positions to a referendum with a vote scheduled for Tuesday April 21, 1998. Staff organized to discuss options, and procedures to save the jobs of the affected staff. I participated in those meetings as a building association representative. However, before the referendum took place, the administration found errors in the state funding source, and the layoffs did not happen.

Politics often runs rampant with deception, ignorance, and cover ups. Here again, I sensed evil at this January Board meeting not long before the proverbial stuff hit the fan.

In February 1998, through an unsolicited mailing, I received a Sacred Heart of Jesus pin. I either set aside or recycle unsolicited mail offerings but, feeling that this one was different; I placed it in a drawer. All the same, the words "This pin is to be worn" echoed in my head, and I wore it to work in hope that it would be a quiet cue to do what Jesus would do. When one prays for patience and endurance, adversity often comes to test your patience.

One afternoon, my neighbor knocked at my back door with a new, black briefcase, telling me she was inspired to give it to me. I had not discussed my work with her, but somehow, she knew. The gift was an ominous warning. I asked, "What do you want of me, Lord? Where do you want me to serve You?" (Luke 18:41).

Gavin De Becker, in his book *The Gift of Fear*[1] posed this question:

> Imagine that all the students are gathered in the auditorium and the Principal surveys the group with this question in mind: who among these students might sexually abuse another child? Through his behavior Joey stands up in the assembly and calls out, it might be me. But the Principal chooses to ignore the boy.

The week before spring break, the staff was handed a puzzle piece. I could tell by their eyes; it was not good news. It involved baseball. A customer relations team and mascot from the local

AAA Baseball League came to advertise their franchise. The marketing team captain read *Casey at Bat*[2] as their mascot danced and performed on stage. The reader cued the kids to shout, "Kill the umpire" as she read the story. The physical education teacher was instructed to tell the staff to encourage the children to interact with the mascot. I told him that I would not instruct my class to shout "Kill the umpire" less than two weeks after the Jonesboro shooting. Was "kill the umpire" rather harsh punishment for missed calls?

Halfway through the reading, my troubled student stood up from his seat in the audience, pointed his hands like a gun and pretended "to take down" the mascot. He was the only one to follow and act out the narrator's refrain of "kill the umpire." News reports often mock discipline of such actions, implicating that young students mean no harm when they act in such a way. That is not true. Not one other student felt compelled to stand up and "kill the umpire." The LRC teacher witnessed this, as did other teachers and the principal. The LRC teacher reached the child first, and her eyes met mine as she told him to sit down and act appropriately. With zero tolerance policies for violent behavior, a child would be removed, at least from the assembly. He, however, remained.

On the following day, the child did not have his bookbag. He told us that his mother had taken it to the principal's office. The next day he was absent and did not return to class until April 22, three days after the spring break ended. Patterns in behavior are critical, and so is notifying the teacher. An unlocked door, a child looking disoriented, angry children at a ball game, a person lurking in a playground—all these may all be pieces to be connected as are the individual and collective behaviors of every living creature. Sometimes we underestimate patterns of behavior.

My district did act on my request. They had a police presence and held a "dog and pony show" involving the crisis intervention team. They were purposely insulting. The CST Director and nurse led the presentation to the children.

If they could take the word of a teacher, then twist it in front of the children, can you imagine what they would do with a child's word? There is warning in the principle advised to me by Pipa, "Children lie as do adults." The children were listening to the adults lie. It is true that liars accuse the innocent of what they themselves are doing. Not all principals are liars, but all liars are unprincipled.

The representative told me not to worry. According to him, since I had not published my memo in a newspaper, I would merely get a "slap on the wrist." When I told my husband, he was naturally alarmed about my job status. I assured him that public behaviors are not confidential and something had to be done.

The representative and I met one time. I did not have a good feeling about him, but I ignored the inner warnings. I thought I was being too suspicious and was not seeing the good in people. I was accused of seeing the negative, or in not being hopeful. I was not discounting my feelings about the representative, but I did not have a lot of options at that point.

I should have gone with my gut feeling about the representative and kept the rose-colored glasses in their pouch. He told me he had worked with the Superintendent before and that his wife was a cousin of the Superintendent's secretary. He meant to comfort me. When his secretary answered the phone, she called me by the Principal's first name. I noted it and sensed something was wrong; but again, I was giving the benefit of the doubt to those who did not deserve it. I could not imagine that everyone had a conspiracy going against me, but I came to understand that, in protecting my interests, other members would have had to answer for violating policies and state law. My representative may have heard from them too.

My inner voice was just preparing me for more turbulent weather ahead. God was guiding me as much as the devil was fighting against me. A storm was brewing, but at least it was not a real bullet fired in my school.

Myth: History does not matter.

CHAPTER 4

FUTURE TEACHER
OF AMERICA—
THE REAR VIEW MIRROR

People see imperfectly, but we do get glimpses of the future from the signals that show up. Living, like driving, requires us to pay attention to the road ahead. Windshields and rearview mirrors help. Looking ahead with a clear view and expectation of what has come before enables discernment.

My twenty-first year of professional work was when I learned what it really meant to be a teacher. I absolutely loved teaching but the people in administration not so much. I had wanted to be a teacher since I was very young. My sisters and I used to set up classrooms for each other—"Stone teacher" was one of our favorite games! We took turns teaching even into adulthood, and four of us entered the educational field. Connect the dots worksheets helped us count and learn the alphabet. Connecting dots is a life skill.

In the 1950s and early 1960s we read stories of Dick, Jane, and their dog, Spot. They liked to run but never once in those stories did the children have to run from their school with their hands up or behind their heads. We had air raid drills but no active shooter drills. We were told the enemy was a foreign nation. Duck and cover was pointless in the early sixties, just as the variation on that technique is not any more useful today.

In fourth grade I saw tears in my teacher's eyes as she spoke with the principal. We were walked into the auditorium on that day in November 1963. The principal walked on stage and announced the assassination of President Kennedy. By the time I attended junior high and high school in Plainfield, NJ, from 1967-1972, we had security guards, policemen and riots. Two more assassinations rocked our youthful existence in 1968. Turbulent times existed in our nation, which spilled into our schools. We could tell what was driving the violence then. What was driving the shootings in the 1990s? What is driving the violence today?

My parents taught us to speak up and debate at the kitchen table with Friday night pizza or Saturday morning hard rolls and coffeecake. My much older siblings loved to debate; little eyes were watching, listening and sometimes interjecting with a comment or two! One day my mom and dad came home from a parent-teacher conference and told me they learned, "Marian needs to speak up more in class." Although I did start to be more vocal, the real moment of truth about my personality came in college after another student took credit and impressed the professor for an idea I had initiated in the small group.

Our neighbor, a wise teacher, gave sage instruction when I was preparing for college. He taught special education and suggested that I obtain my elementary certification, then pursue special education. My undergraduate degree in Psychology with Elementary Education certification was followed by my graduate degree in Special Education. My practice teaching was in first grade. As an undergrad I volunteered, worked in a private special school, and substituted in special education classes before getting employed full time.

I did appreciate my time at a school in Williamsport, PA, working one summer as an aide in a Pre-K setting. Kathleen and all the other children contributed to my experience: Kathleen with Down's syndrome was a spitfire and stole everyone's heart. In the summer program, living in a tent for one week with two teenagers classified as profoundly retarded (before those classifications were changed), helped me experience living close up with non-verbal children.

I had my fair share of experiences with special needs children. In an Intermediate Unit class, we had to feed Arnie, who made sure the green beans were delivered back to the spoon. I stopped a "runner" from escaping one day while substituting. It was truly gut instinct to stop him. A situation like that happened years later when I was setting up for an Art Goes to School presentation; as the child was running away from the school, I called his name, and he stopped long enough for the aide to catch up.

As my first professional experience, I worked in a developmental preschool. "Betty Barracuda," her nickname in the district, led the CST. I soon learned I walked into the churning relationship waters of a great preschool teacher, a barracuda, and a bull in a china shop (the superintendent). What is it about barracudas in education? You find that politics mixes in everything and personal discord is in every profession.

The Principal of an elementary school, looking for innovative, younger teachers, asked that I apply for a first-grade position. I spent weekends at the school getting it ready for the week, while my husband put construction paper on many bulletin boards. That Principal later became Superintendent in the community where we lived. I hated the first few weeks of that first year where I just could not seem to light a spark. It was in September, when the first-grade classes took a trip to the Philadelphia Zoo, that I fell in love. They were so well behaved and enjoyed themselves. I bought unlined index cards and invested in reward stickers, printed "The Greatest" and put a sticker on each card. At the end of each day, each student received one. A few years later, a boy who was then in fifth grade, told me he still had those sticker cards. I could not wait to return on Monday mornings.

I organized large groups, small groups and learning stations. One veteran teacher referred to my class teaching style, as "organized chaos." I worked two years in the first grade, then a reduction in force (RIF) sent me kicking to the LRC. That experience and having to work with one eighth grader at the local parochial school in that district made me realize that change is good. More teachers should welcome the transfers as long as they do not professionally hurt or humiliate them. The children in the LRC did make me feel like dancing for three years.

It was in the very early eighties in a resource room long, long ago, that I was "shot" with a video game stylus shaped like a gun. It was used with Pong, an Atara game released in 1975 to be played using the television. An innocent game of table tennis, the game helped with eye-hand coordination and reaction time. I used it as a reward on Friday afternoons if the children would spend that time on activities outside the classroom; this could be a relaxed and productive time.

Was it in 1980, that the world was on edge to find out "Who shot J.R. Ewing?" in the Friday night drama on CBS, Dallas 1980. I was. I had not wanted the shooter to be Bobby or J.R.'s wife. Our inside joke became, "Who shot Mrs. Carlino?" I laughed and let the kids continue to play the game. No one got sent home, no notes were penned hastily, no punishment. It was a game. There was no history of physical outbursts from the child. Forty-three years later I still remember that child's name and face with joy. I remember how the principal in that elementary school came to get that same television in 1981, when a mentally ill man shot President Reagan. The shooting of a President is rare, but the event impacts the immediate moments and so many moments for years after. With the many shootings in 1996-1998, I absolutely guarantee my reaction would not have been so chill. I absolutely guarantee, I would not have had a video game with a gun shaped stylus.

In 1983, after five and a half years in one school, I left my tenured status to try out new interests in education. I enrolled in Occupational Therapy coursework at my local community college; worked in a group home with cognitively impaired adult men; secured a large contract as a plant manager for adults with disabilities before I left that position due to the long commute. I then took a job with at-risk youth, including gang members, and employment challenged adults older than fifty-five with offices in three counties. I was never afraid of the youth bringing a weapon into the class. At one point, members of opposing gangs were in the same group.

It was not because I was naïve to the situations, but boundaries may have been more defined in the early 1980s. Neighborhoods and city limits were well defined and named; some you knew to just stay out of. Pleasantville youth were more likely to go into Atlantic City than the reverse. For the adults seeking re-employment, territories existed. Southern New Jersey was a resort area that closed up in the off-season months and hired seasonal workers. It was a way of life in that region for many years. Cape May County, at the southern end of New Jersey, had rural areas and beach communities. One man told me, "Anything north of Dias Creek was north Jersey to him." This man lived in the southernmost region of NJ. His perspective of north Jersey was at the border of Cape May County. The nuances of students are details worth noting at any age.

In 1987-88, I accepted a position in a school setting to have a more reasonable work schedule after the birth of my daughter. I substituted in a self-contained seventh and eighth grade resource room for seven months. That group had emotional challenges (not disclosed before I took the job). One eighth grade boy reacted to a backfire from a car that passed the trailer, telling me that the bomb had detonated early. The Principal walked in that day when I was yelling at the student and it was the student who was suspended, not me. In that case, the parents could not have been more on board. There were no formal incident reports then. But the threat to a staff member—even if just implied or veiled—was taken seriously.

In 1988, I left full time work to spend more time with my daughter, taking a part time position in the district. I worked as a Supplemental teacher with K-3 and then part time as the Learning Resource Center teacher until I was hired full time in the LRC before transferring into the second-grade position.

For two years under one Principal, we teamed as units and used thematic teaching. As the resource room teacher, I coordinated activities to what the regular classes were doing. We had fun and innovative ideas. One year, my LRC was a theater company. We performed skits and created videos for family visitors. Our hallways were alive with children's work. I played the role of a teacher who needed a vacation in a school wide play production—perhaps a prophetic role because eventually I would get one! However, all thematic plans were scrapped when Pipa became the principal.

In my last year in the resource room, I worked in the morning in the primary LRC and in the early afternoon with the middle school students. Adapting curriculum is key and I excelled at that, putting in more direct time with the students than the full-time teacher. I liked to name my classes, so in 1996-97, when I transferred into the second-grade position, I named them the "Beautiful Butterflies." I chose that name to honor my mom who had died in 1981. They certainly lived up to their name as beautiful children. We released butterflies as a year-end activity, and even though the summer break had just begun, the families participated. For the 1997-98 year, I named the students "Courageous Cats." I chose that name in memory of my dad. The cat is my dad's symbol. Raising children with my mother from 1934-1974, I would say he was courageous.

I was not a fan of inclusion as a resource room teacher because of how it was implemented. I may have been shown the door a lot sooner had this poem been published in 1995 when I first submitted it.

In class support is the trend today, improve self-esteem is what they say. Do not pull out, go in instead. Standby at the ready to repeat what is said. Keep the children all on task. Have them do what the teacher asks. Keep the children working on the same skill. Because in class support is the new magic pill. Do not let the children see we are not all the same; that seems to be the rule of this game. Everyone, solve these problems and read this book. Oh, if saying this was all it took. Providing what is said is relevant or not, make sure the children are on the right spot.

I did not pull out. I went in instead at the ready to repeat what was said. I kept the children right on task. I made them do what the teacher asked. I kept the children on the same skill because in-class support is the new magic pill. I tried not to show that we are not all the same. I knew those were the rules of the game. Self-esteem is important; this I know. With in-class support, we should see it grow. But is self-esteem built by being treated the same, or by being treasured for differences, regardless of name? So, a firm supporter of in-class support I am not, because it is difficult for all to stand on one spot. Some may agree, others may boil, but in-class support can be like mixing oil and water. While some children may rise up, it is the drowning of others that needs to be stopped. I see in-class support as a cost-saving device, with our children the ones paying the price.

I wrote my observations through this little poem, because I am sure my opinions were sure to hit home. With whole language adapted to a whole group approach, many missed out on the one-on-one or small group working environment. I did not want all to be on the same spot. However, page sharing with adults for safety should be a required skill.

My years of experience taught me that teaching is an emotional and time-consuming line of work. But teaching was my way of life and I spent hours beyond the normal workday, and much of my money on supplies. My entire volunteer commitment was in educating the young person. Days off coincided with my children's days off, and summer break I spent with my family. Life was good.

As I did every July, I started preparing in earnest for the group of second graders who would become "mine." The Chinese folk tale, *The Empty Pot*, would be our theme story for the year. Is it any coincidence I received the most perceptive advice of my life at a Chinese restaurant in 1998? Preparation for the first few days took weeks. Welcome notes were written and sent with a play on words from the New Jersey slogan, "Courageous Cats, Puurfect Together." I had wondered aloud to the LRC teacher before the start of school if I could love this group as much as I had loved the children in my 1996-97 year. Life is full of teachable moments.

The book *Random Acts of Kindness* encourages grace through the smallest gestures, and I rewarded kind efforts. The golden rule works.

Inclusion was trending as it continues to do so. My class would be considered the inclusion class, as it was the previous year. However, trends, as we see in recent history, are not always best practices and can exclude the very people the experts claim it will benefit. Trendy leads to a one-size-fits–all mentality, which can give rise to collateral damage.

I sent the following letter to the parents' homes. Welcome to the second-grade class of Carlino's Courageous Cats!

Second grade is an exciting time for the children, teachers, and parents! This is the time the children, teachers, and parents start seeing the fruits of their labor and the TLC given in kindergarten and first grade. The students acquire new responsibilities. Independent work becomes a regular activity. Children will lead small group discussions, referred to as literature circles. Roles for members of literature circles are well defined. Facilitators, recorders, and reporters are titles given to children who present the information orally to the group.

Daily, we have sharing time. News related to our studies may be shown or discussed. However, it is not show and tell. I do encourage the children to talk in front of the large group at this time, because it may be the only time when the child has the opportunity to tell me something special!

While sharing news is optional, getting up in front of the group or answering questions is not. I try to reach even the shy child daily. As the year progresses, even those who are hesitant in the beginning, will open up. I do not feel it does justice to children to let them pass up an opportunity to tell others what they are thinking about a particular situation.

I readily admit that I make mistakes, so mistakes are no big thing. We learn from them! The children need to see that it is OK if the effort to try their best is involved.

We have great support when it comes to teachers who will be in the class daily helping the children. Small group instruction, which is flexible, is the rule when helpers are in. Mrs. K is the chief cook. We relate all food activities to stories or to special occasions and call it "Cooking with Mrs. K."

All reading and language arts skills are integrated through the theme approach using the literature text. Science and social studies are incorporated into the study of the stories. This class will not be following the publisher's order exactly step by step. I like my way better! We do move around the texts. Social studies and science texts become reference resources! I do follow the guidelines for math. Enrichment activities are provided as much as possible for those children who are moving more rapidly through the skills. As part of my professional improvement plan this year, I have chosen to correspond with families monthly through newsletters. Look for "Cat Prints"; we will all be sticking our paws in the ink!

This letter was not brought in as evidence at the hearing. At the hearing, Pipa told the Board that it was standard operating procedure for all teachers to have correspondence approved to send home, and I had violated that rule. Of course, my letter to her during the dispute was not sent to parents, so it did not violate her special rule for me.

This was my submission for the November 5, 1997, newsletter, which did not make it to the discussion on April 20,1998 either. September, October, November and then, makes no difference what group we're in. General Assembly or committees at work, second grade has a lot of company perks. Reading and writing, spelling and math, we all travel down the educational path. Stories of families and friendships abound, where brave and honest characters can be found. To practice math facts, around the world we go. We always choose to answer to show what we know! In Art and PE, we do muscle motor things, but music allows our hearts to sing. Cooking with Mrs. K and computers too, we have a lot of fun in whatever we do! Color the flower for kind acts that are done, play at recess in the bright yellow sun. Happy with options, choices galore. We'd like more time to work and explore. Cheers for the teamwork and tips of our hats, because we are a class act of Courageous Cats!

I am not sure which of the two parent letters Pipa found offensive from September1997.

By the way, the name, "Courageous Cats," turned out to be a prophetic name for the group that year, and for me. Each experience has added to the fabric of my existence.

THE SOLEMN SANHEDRIN

On the day before spring break, on April 8, 1998, I received an offer I could not refuse to a hearing on Monday evening following the holiday. With the vacation, there was no time to meet again with the association representative.

Please give rise that pursuant to N. J. S. A. 10: 4-12 B (8), you are hereby advised that the special meeting of the Board of Education will be held on April 20, 1998, at 7:00 p.m. The Board will schedule a disciplinary hearing regarding your professional performance. Discussion will take place in closed session unless you deliver a written request to the Business Administrator/ Board Secretary that you wish such discussion would be held in a public session. Final action that may affect you, may or may not take place at that time.

Once scheduled, it was to have been advertised as an "open meeting" through Sunshine Law requirements. Where were the people for the open session?

I trusted in the integrity of the Board members and in the system designed to provide due process for the employees, as guaranteed in state tenure laws. Tenure status is not a job for life. Implementation of laws depends upon the honesty of the players. Alone, except for the representative, I thought I was prepared. I remained focused and strong, wearing my Sacred Heart of Jesus pin, not as a good luck charm, but as a reminder.

Before entering the meeting, the representative and I met for only the second time. He told me that he "forgot more about school law than the School Board attorney knew." Now I was alarmed. He recommended that I must promote myself to the BOE. On that point, he was right. Although I had worked for the district for almost ten years, they did not know me except for one time when they heard me defend the jobs for the aides. The reader, in fact, knows more of my history than they did after ten years. I should have chosen to keep the proceedings open. However, that procedure was not explained, and I was not counseled that I could have had witnesses speak on my behalf. I was not informed ahead of time either that the mother and the advocate would be allowed to speak, although she chose not to.

So, on April 20, 1998, I sat and listened to the voices of discontent in a closed-door recorded hearing. The administrator and Board attorney had an agenda: the mother and the advocate were sitting in the board office. The Principal, Pipa, and I were sworn in to tell the truth.

The Board followed a chronology presented by the Principal. Everyone acknowledged that information she presented from September 1997 and a letter from the CST were not in my file that morning. Pipa began her submission by making unfounded derogatory statements about my performance dating back a few years and my not being "brought along."

It is a teacher who I am trying to help come along with us, to fit into the philosophy of the public schools and, unfortunately, I do not know if Mrs. Carlino has the ability to be remediated to do that. I do not know. ... However, it was always a struggle. You have some teachers who come along and follow your lead, and you have some teachers that you really have to work hard to bring along. Now, I will tell you the truth. I switched her from the LRC to a classroom position because I had so much trouble in my mind. Not enough to document, not enough, but and it's not in here, so it's not part of it. But I will tell you that in her position as an LRC teacher, I was concerned that

33

the children were not getting everything that they needed. So that's why I thought, let me give her a classroom with not all of Special Ed. Special Ed children are very, very difficult. It's a tough, I think it's tough. I'm not saying difficult discipline wise. I'm saying it is a challenging position, sometimes more so than having a full class. So, I thought, let me try Mrs. Carlino in a regular classroom. But not enough to document. Just enough to try her somewhere else.

She then explained to the Board that the child has special rights.

I know Special Education law. I know the fact that needless public labeling is very, very serious. I wondered at that point if remediation was possible for Mrs. Carlino ... As a classified special education child, yes, some special rights, and the individualized education plan spells out a program, and we cannot deviate from that program.

The principal then accused me of breaking a "needless public labeling law." But no lawyer or a search of state statutes could define such a law. The classification in emotional disorders factors into discipline. Learning right from wrong should not be connected to the emotional ability of any individual. I do not believe in zero tolerance or one-size-fits-all discipline.

Pipa also dismissed the boy's behavior on March 24 as being my fault. There was a part in here where she said,

I took the word of the child over her. There was no issue of that. This was never about the child, and I never discussed anything. I never said anything to him: "that your teacher did a bad thing today" or anything like that. However, in my heart I knew, when I took him back, he had not done anything wrong when she sent him down.

In addition, my use of the term "strike" was twisted during Pipa's testimony. The Board members and the association representative had some playful banter about baseball during the questioning. Pipa explained,

I have never heard of anything like that, and I was very shaken by thinking that a child could be struck out. To me it's a baseball term. It has negative connotations. And that is why I had a conference with the teacher and said, "Listen. There's a Lee Canter Approach of Progressive Discipline, which we used in the other first grade. Talk to Mrs. N. to see what she does. Let's see if we can't lighten this up a little."

Pipa explained under oath about the other teachers' rights to know about the child's issues.

That's why only the teacher who works with the child, should see his or her records and is to be privy to them. There is no reason for the teachers, such as the special subject teachers, to know. They are seated in a meeting with the CST at the beginning of the year and told just as much as they need to know about this child or any other special education child. We do not tell them anything more than they need to know to be successful with the child. So, for her to have revealed the distress in the family that came out in a Child Study Team meeting, a confidential meeting, where the parent knows she has the right to share and it will never be taken out of the room, I would say that the statement that she repeated which the mother said was totally out of context and so did the other two people—out of context—the way it was said here is very damaging.

When asked about the boy's access to guns, Pipa said,

We're all aware that he and his dad are active in that. But if Mrs. Carlino would have asked, he plays the drums in those reenactments. He does not carry a gun.

To rebut this assertion, I did not pull "access to guns" out of thin air. The child was very excited and proud of his participation in the Civil War re-enactment group. He brought pictures to show himself dressed in uniform and holding a gun. Do you know that antique guns still fire? Within that year, there were news reports of people getting shot at reenactments. Do you know that shooting a blank at close range to the head can kill? Do you know when a gun is real or a toy? I can definitely answer the first two questions. The third one, not even policemen can tell the difference at times.

Then the Board attorney spoke. He compared me to a priest and a rabbi.

> The thing that I find most disturbing is I don't hear—even though the words were said—I don't see them backed up with action on the part of the teacher ... that there is really remorse about sending this letter, and there is an appreciation on the part of this teacher in terms of the impact that sending this letter has not only on this child and this child's parents, but also in terms of the integrity of the entire system ... I would be expected to understand that the integrity of the system, the foundation of the system with the ability of the parents to come in and spill their guts out. Now, I think in Mrs. Carlino's case you hold her to a higher standard because she is not just an ordinary teacher, she is a teacher that has a special education certification ... This is almost like a professional situation where you, maybe go to a priest or rabbi and you confide in them, knowing that whatever you are saying within that room is not going to leave the four corners of that room ... We have a parent out there who feels that in this case of her child that confidence is shattered, and any other parent who gets wind of this incident, I think, has to come to the same conclusion.

The Board would soon find out what the other parents were feeling.

Myth: Teachers cannot share information with other teachers.

When it was my turn, I read a story first before responding to all questions.

Most children's stories are meant for adults. What kind of seeds do we plant? The seed that falls on good ground will yield a fruitful harvest. Gardening is an art form. People look for the beautiful artwork of nature; we look for visible signs that we are doing the right thing. Story telling is also an art form. What can Ping's gardening technique teach?

The Empty Pot[3]

A long time ago in China, there was a boy named Ping who loved flowers. Anything he planted burst into bloom. Up came flowers, bushes, and even big fruit trees as if by magic. Everyone in the kingdom loved flowers too. They planted them everywhere and the air smelled like perfume. The Emperor loved birds and animals but flowers most of all, and he tended his own garden every day.

But the Emperor was very old. He needed to choose a successor to the throne. Who would be his successor? And how would the Emperor choose? Because the Emperor loved flowers so much, he decided to let the flowers choose.

The next day a proclamation was issued. All the children in the land were to come to the palace; there they would be given special flower seeds by the Emperor, "Whoever can show me their best in a year's time,' he said, 'will succeed me to the throne."

This news created great excitement throughout the land. Children from all over the country swarmed to the palace to get their flower seed. All the parents wanted their children to be chosen Emperor, and all the children hoped they would be chosen too. When Ping received his flower seed from the Emperor, he was the happiest child of all. He was sure he could grow the most beautiful flowers.

Ping filled a flowerpot with rich soil. He planted the seed in it very carefully. He watered it every day. He could not wait to see it sprout, grow, and blossom into a beautiful flower. Day after day passed, but nothing grew in the pot.

Ping was worried. He put new soil into a bigger pot. Then he transferred the seed into the rich black soil. Another few months he waited. Still, nothing happened.

By and by, the whole year passed. Spring came and all the children put on their best clothes to meet the emperor. They rushed to the palace with their beautiful flowers eagerly hoping to be chosen. Ping was ashamed of his empty pot. He thought the other children would laugh at him because for once he could not get a flower to grow. His clever friend ran by holding a great big plant. "Ping," he said, "You are not really going to the emperor with an empty pot, are you? Couldn't you grow a big flower like mine?" "I have grown lots of flowers better than yours," Ping said. "It's just this seed that won't grow." Ping's father overheard this and said, "You did your best, and your best is good enough to present to the emperor." Holding the empty pot in his hands, he went straightaway to the palace.

The emperor was looking at the flowers slowly, one by one. How beautiful all the flowers were! But the Emperor was frowning and did not say a word. Finally, he came to Ping. Ping hung his head in shame, expecting to be punished. The emperor asked him, "Why did you bring an empty pot?" Ping started to cry and replied, "1 planted the seed that you gave me, and I've watered it every day, but it didn't sprout. I tended it all year long, but nothing grew. So, today, I had to bring an empty pot without a flower. It was the best I could do."

When the Emperor heard these words, a smile slowly spread over his face, and he put his arm around Ping. Then he explained to one and all, "I have found him. I have found the person worthy of being Emperor. Where you got your seeds from, I do not know. But the seeds I gave you had all been cooked, so it was impossible for any of them to grow. I admire Ping's great courage to appear before me with the empty pot, and now I reward him with my kingdom and make him Emperor of all the land."

What kind of seeds was being planted and watered?

The representative and I waited for the Board's announcement in the cafeteria. The mother, the advocate and the principal sat together on the left side, looking quite smug as they faced the Board of Education table. The representative and I sat on the right. He had told me I did not have to stay. Why would I leave? I had the right to be there and had done nothing wrong. The subject was me, so why not hear what the jury and judge had decided?

After a break, during which Barracuda advised the Board of their options, the meeting was called back to order at 11:10 p.m. The roll call commenced, and all the formal announcements cleared before a BOE member made a motion to take a vote. Looking at the faces, I could see they believed me. But the set agenda had been executed; with a barracuda in the water, the sharks had company.

The union representative was even shocked at how long the meeting lasted.

Let the minutes reflect that the meeting reopened to the public at approximately 11:10 p.m. M. Carlino 1.2. Moved by Mrs. K, seconded by Mr. C, to withhold the 1998-99 increment from Marian Carlino. A roll call voted indicated 8 yes, zero no. Motion carried.

I was disappointed by the decision to penalize me. I believed the resolution would favor me, but that is not what their plan entailed. Upon further inquiry by my representative to the attorney, he said my increment might be susceptible to lifetime removal.

In conversation with an acquaintance later that year, I asked about the Board's lawyer. The acquaintance used the term "barracuda" to describe him. So, I was swimming with barracudas while sharks roamed the water. I identified myself as shark bait to the representative. "Barracuda" was a good nickname for him and Jezebel for the Superintendent. I have referred to the Principal as "Pipa."

Standing in the darkness by my car after the meeting, we waited as the participants walked past us. They could not look at me, especially the advocate. Months later, in November, at the meetings held at the NJ Teachers' Convention where I sought answers and brought my children with me. I saw the advocate. She saw me, cringed, and left. As I walked up to her booth, another woman stood there when I asked if they advocated for what was best for the child or what the parents wanted. She could not answer.

Advocating for what is best for the child and what is best for the parents is not always the same thing. These people knew that. When you destroy another person's livelihood and reputation, that person would be hard to forget. Because the advocate wrote for a statewide advocacy organization, I contacted them and met with the County Superintendent. The advocate was a Board of Education member for the Special Services School District and had broad access and influence. The Advocacy organization and the School District Superintendent needed to know how she was using her influence.

In the testimony, Pipa had (ironically) mentioned the Lee Canter approach to classroom discipline. Lee Canter was a social worker, who developed techniques in the 1970s which were popular in the late 1990s. I did use his approach of standing near or next to the disruptive student when instructing the large group. In an overview of his book, he ascertained that teachers should be in charge of the classroom.

This method teaches that the teacher has a "right" to decide what is best for his or her students. Teachers should determine what is best for all students and then expect compliance. The main axiom of this method is that no student should ever prevent a teacher from teaching or keep another student from learning, period. In order to achieve this axiom, teachers must behave assertively, not aggressively or passively. They must be consistently assertive in their wants and expected behavior in the classroom. This works well, because the students see the teacher is firmly requesting a standard of behavior, and that he or she is going to take assertive steps to ensure that students respect their wishes. This method has the teacher giving clear, firm direction, which, if followed, is met with positive reinforcement; if not followed, the undesired behavior is met with negative consequences. Students are not viewed as enemies and are not treated with a hostile or sarcastic attitude. Rather, students are viewed as allies who are expected to cooperate for the good of all. Teachers who have adopted this method say it is easy to use and implement. Having the ability to be assertive is key to this method. If you are a teacher who is not assertive, a course on assertiveness may be of assistance to you.

From Universal Class https://www.universalclass.com /articles/self-help/types-of-classroom-managementassertive discipline.htm#:~:text=Assertive%20discipline%20was%20 a%20system%20developed%20by%20Lee,classroom%20in%20 which%20the%20teacher%20is%20in%20charge

Myth: People tell the truth when sworn in.

BENCHED

"For a day in your courts is better than one thousand in the courts of man. I would rather be a doorkeeper in the House of my God than to dwell in the tents of wickedness" (Psalm 84:10).

Jesus tells us that the truth will set you free. It set me free all right. I told my husband that the Board withheld my increment, but I still had my job. I was grateful that I had the opportunity to speak.

April 21, 1998, I drove to work, stopping at Our Lady of Sorrows to pray. Without God, getting through the day would be a challenge. Not only was I upset, but I was physically exhausted from the late night before. I am resilient and a fighter, so I was prepared for the next shoe," at least for that day, still sporting rose-colored glasses. Are we not taught to see the best in people and to forgive? I offered forgiveness for the written reprimand just as I had to forgive the people on the Board. "Father forgive them they do not know what they do" is what Jesus said at the cross (Luke 23:34). I pitied them.

I confided in only one teacher about my increment decided publicly because I was under the impression that closed-door meetings were confidential. I had been accused of breaking confidentiality, so I was not willing to give them more ammunition to use against me. One Board member told a source, "She handled herself well in the meeting." I had nothing to hide but the Board accomplished breaking the confidential nature of the meeting.

That day I also received a note stating that I had to meet with the administration. The local association President was my witness. I had started refusing to meet at any point with any administrator without someone being present. In March, the middle school Principal ran interference when I tried to meet with the local President; even the Superintendent was upset about that. The civics teacher who held public office tried to interfere, and not to my advantage. He made a sarcastic comment directed right at me in the teachers' lunchroom about sitting in the Jesus corner because of my pin and concerns.

Aware that the state Test of Cognitive Skills, a standardized test, had to be administered, with the disturbed student absent, the class was peaceful. I did not want them distracted. Children are perceptive, and people were already discussing the Board hearing.

Then the call came to meet with the Superintendent and the Principal. The Superintendent informed me that they had decided to remove me so that the child's educational plan could remain in place. They interpreted the law to mean the child had the right to be there, but I did not. The administration did this at great risk of lawsuits from others. I was offered three choices: take a position as the basic skills teacher, which was budgeted part time, take sick leave, or take family medical leave. Family medical leave is without pay, and I did not want to take a demotion. The administration had selected my replacement, so I was effectively "out of there." I had accrued sixty days of sick time but had to make the decision to take sick leave after consulting with my husband since I did not want it to be a unilateral choice. We, the Superintendent, principal and the local president and I were to meet again on April 22.

I returned to my room somewhat numb but managed to administer the test with the basic skills teacher. The administration trusted me to give that test with a level head after questioning my skills, and within minutes of demoting me. I maintained my composure, with an occasional trembling in my voice as I read directions.

As the students lined up at the end of the day, one student asked if I was still their teacher. So, the parent chose to blast the request. Other professionals could break confidentiality, but I was the only one to be brought before the BOE.

Before I left for the day, coworkers came to offer prayers and sympathy. The time to speak would have been on or before April 20 but no one offered to speak up for me. Martin Luther King once said, "It is the silence of your friends when an enemy attacks that will be remembered."

No one recognized the administrative retaliatory actions as illegal and in direct violation of NJ law. The silence was deafening. The code of silence is alive and well in all areas of life, and education is not immune. Some may call it self- preservation until a shooting happens, then what is the intimidated into silence called?

Myth: Silence is golden.

Evicted from My Classroom

On the morning of April 22, after I drove my children to their school, I made a visit to Our Lady of Sorrows to pray in front of the Blessed Sacrament. It had become a daily stop, so I arrived later than the 7:30 a.m. time that my coworkers had expected. Prayer was essential. I felt that the news would only get worse. God gives us the gift of intuition, but we need to pray and listen to our hearts and His voice. I was told that a substitute would be in my room, but when I arrived, no substitute was in sight. The Principal said I should have called for one and sent me back to the classroom to work. She was clearly lying.

In line, at the classroom door, was the child. I had not done anything to him, so I welcomed him and all the children into the class prepared to teach. At 8:35 a.m. the rose-colored glasses had to come off again. Pipa told me to get out. In shock I looked at her and asked, "May I get my purse?" How ridiculous! Those are the only words that came to mind. So, I stepped into the hallway as directed without my pocketbook, asking myself where to go. Of course, this was against policy even for children, for no child could be sent into the hallway for discipline.

After standing there trying to get my bearings, I decided to go to the front office to sit. I reasoned that, if they were looking for me, I would have to be available, plus I wanted witnesses. What could they do next? While sitting there, I saw the boy's mother walk out of the Superintendent's office in her police uniform. Did she have a gun? She was a dispatcher for a local township police force. She had that same blank stare on her face as she did on April 20.

The meeting to discuss my decision was postponed until 1:00 p.m. They were good at their craft as were Pontius Pilate, Herod, and the Romans. They kept me three to four hours in the belly of the whale waiting like Jonah—or were they really the Sanhedrin? Believe me, when the Scriptures from Lent leading up to Easter are all about rejection and betrayal, I did see some similarities. Most of the morning, I waited in the office. From the staff reactions, one would think I had leprosy. The local television station was doing a remote from the school. I thought about going public at once, but it could only make matters worse. Who would have been brave enough to witness for me? Were the staff possibly in shock?

While I was waiting to meet with the Superintendent to tell her my decision, the Principal was directing the LRC teacher to take notes as she told the children I had gotten a promotion. Children are young, but not stupid.

When the LRC teacher took the children for a walk, I collected belongings. I completed plans for the new teacher and, with the help of the basic skills teacher, put names on the standardized achievement tests. I advised her that teachers did need to examine the violence because more would happen. She took over the next year in my second-grade class. I decorated the room's windows with large garden flags, changing one flag to a giant red rose. Maybe I was channeling Ping. Except for a few personal items, I left all my teaching supplies. This action was met with an attempted slap in the face several months later.

At 1:00 p.m., I met with the Superintendent. I did break down at the meeting and told her that I could not take it anymore. I said

I would be taking sick leave, not wanting to feed into the lies told about me anymore. I left that day in tears in no condition to say goodbye to anyone, nor was I allowed to. As I left the building, I just kept walking straight to my car. Not wanting to turn into a pillar of salt, I resolved to shake the dust from my shoes. God was leading me forward. "Those who go forth weeping, carrying the seeds to be sown, they will come back rejoicing carrying their sheaths" (Psalm 126:6).

I drove straight home and curled up on the sofa until it was time to pick up my children from the after-school program. For the next two days, except for my husband, I told no one. That night, as a family unit in my children's school, though with me still in shock, we stood up for teachers whose positions were on the Board's cutting list. The fate of the gifted and talented program teacher was why we were there. My husband and daughter spoke as my son, and I stood with them. If I had opened my mouth, my voice would have been cracking with tears.

Stress levels are indicative of trouble. I had no physical pain, but I was uneasy about behaviors and worried daily that someone would be hurt. I warned my children at home that I would not tolerate what I had to deal with concerning the boy, so I took my feelings home with me and that affected my family. My stress levels were high because of the child, but the Principal played a significant role in that. Educators take on levels of stress as normal and account for it as just part of the job. In the meantime, we miss warning signs. Children deal with stress with varying degrees of success depending on resiliency. We have seen the extreme failures as children take vengeance on others and in suicides. The kindergarten teacher had once shared with me the strife she'd had two years earlier; she stressed out, as did his first-grade teacher.

My doctor wrote a letter for me about an acute stress reaction allowing me to take the rest of the year off, using forty sick days.

I was still trying to discern what to do. Since my children were finishing their standardized tests, my husband and I decided not to tell them. The decision was already public, and I would not answer calls because of confidentiality and legal misgivings. I was on a new path, but I did not exactly know why or where I was going.

Psalm 56:11 says, "In God have I put my trust: I will not be afraid what man can do unto me." With courage we act, even with real fears. I had absolutely experienced this and felt fear. The parents did too. But acting in spite of it, we have our responsibility as parents and teachers. I owned both roles.

On April 22, 1998, the parents of all the children received a letter inviting them to a meeting on Friday April 24. In the meeting, they would learn the reason for my leaving, according to the spin. It added, "Refreshments will be served." Was it a wake? I had not been informed but God showed me the letters that were left in the room. I should have been invited.

I did not think that principles could sink any lower until I received a certified letter on April 24. It was from the BOE explaining in numbered paragraphs why they had voted to remove my increment and then remove me from my class. I told my husband it held clues that would back me up and defend my convictions. However, it would take months for my head to clear enough for me to figure out how.

April 22, 1998

Dear Mrs. Carlino: This is to advise you that the Board of Education, as a result of a hearing which was conducted on April 20, 1998, unanimously voted to withhold your employment increment. The reasons and the basis for this action were set forth in the hearing and include, but are not limited to, the following incidents which occurred on September 25, 1997, and September 29,1997, which demonstrated your failure to follow procedures and an insensitivity to the needs of a child. Those incidents resulted in written warnings to you from your Principal. An incident occurring on or about March 24, 1998, in which you failed to demonstrate sensitivity to a child's needs, failed to exhibit minimum levels of competence, and failed to follow procedures resulted in a written warning to you from your Principal. See a letter that you sent dated March 25, 1998, which contained sensitive, confidential information concerning the child and the child's family and contains unjustifiable inflammatory comments in regard and disregard of the rights of the child and family, the letter was distributed in numerous employees in the district. Taken individually and collectively, the Board decided that those incidents demonstrated incompetence and insensitivity on your part and a failure to follow procedures and other requirements. In taking this action, the Board is relying on the evidence and information presented during the three and a half hour hearing which was held on April 20, 1998. A copy of this letter will be placed in your personnel file.

Sincerely, The Business Administrator, copy to Superintendent and personnel file.

On the night of April 24, a student in Edinburgh Pennsylvania brought a gun to a dance and killed a male teacher at point blank range. The teacher was well liked and respected in his district, according to news reports.

I was starting to get a clearer view of my future. What the caterpillar thought was the end of life, the butterfly realized was just the beginning.

IMMEDIATE AFTERMATH

With the number of shootings in 1997, one would think every teacher would have written a letter. Instead, we were forbidden from discussing such things. Shannon Wright's death was a wakeup call for me. While I woke up, others shut their eyes and hardened their hearts: "It could not happen here. What was I thinking?"

After April 24 and April 26, still feeling the sting of humiliation, I only spoke to two close friends. Not sure of what to say or do, I asked my friends what they would expect from their children's teachers under the circumstances? They said they would want to hear from the teacher. One woman, who called, worked with me in the church religious education program. She left a kind message expressing the parents' sentiments for more dialogue with me.

That weekend, we traveled to my mother-in-law's home. My husband's niece was born on April 22, so we wanted to meet the baby. I told my mother-in-law the whole episode and asked her to pray for the truth to come out. She started praying the Rosary for me. There is a church named Saint Catherine of Sienna near her home where we enjoyed Mass whenever we visited. On that Sunday April 26, as I read the church bulletin, the words "courage of your convictions" jumped out at me.

Author, Timothy McCanna, wrote:

Courage in the line of duty, whether it be in battle, in firefighting, or in protecting the public against criminal violence,

49

is admired by most of us. There are other acts of courage, however. They may not attract the same attention, but they are equally admirable ... There is the person standing up to public or private ridicule in defense of his or her beliefs. Going against public opinion can often be more difficult than physical fighting.[4]

I finally explained to my children my job status or lack of. Admittedly, I was far from cool and collected when I broke the news to them. With nerves frayed and children misbehaving, the words just did not come out the way I expected. But my daughter's reaction reflected just what I would have said to her if she had been reprimanded. "What did you do?" she exclaimed. I told her that I had done my job as expected, but that the administration did not like it. My husband and children were loyal but naturally worried. I earned 50% of the household income and held the health insurance. I did, however, reassure them that our faith in God would see us through.

My coworker who demanded that the same child be taken out of her class the previous year was also an active member in her faith practice. She told me that when she heard the Good Shepherd Gospel at her church service on April 26, she thought of me. Good shepherds lay down their lives for their flock. I appreciated the comparison, although I was not feeling all that good. I wondered whether I was a good shepherd or a Judas. I preferred to use the analogy with my kids of the good witch or the bad witch in *The Wizard of Oz*, the Frank L. Baum story told in the 1939 movie by Metro Goldwyn Mayer. I called myself Glinda, but at times, Mrs. Gulch. and her alter ego, the wicked witch, were applied.

I learned that my absence from school was being treated as a crisis, as if I had died. The children were upset and confused; the parents were angry. On April 24, they learned that my dismissal centered on the boy. The wise ones did not believe the spin. Others were just bewildered and upset because their normal had been disrupted.

Not sure how to advise, for two weeks I prayed and found a Scripture passage that gave me confidence, Luke 21:12-15:

> But before any of this, they will manhandle and persecute you summoning you to synagogues and prisons bringing you to trial before kings and governors all because of my name. You will be brought to give witness on account of it. I bid you resolve not to worry about your defense beforehand, for I will give you words and wisdom which none of your adversaries can take exception to or contradict (Eastern Catholic Church translation).

Prayer led me to action, but not before the local weekly newspaper ran a story about me as the parents addressed their concerns about the events at the Board meeting held in early May 1998. I found the answer in the article. Although the reporter never reached out to me before publishing the piece, she had done me a favor. A closed door opened, and I was now free to walk through it. I had to ease the distress for the parents and let the children know I was OK. I called one parent to say that I would be at the next open session to speak. She said she would reach out to other parents. I called one teacher who told other staff members. Rumors flew. Some had allegiance to the Child Study Team; others were just scared and ill informed.

Up to this point, the staff thought I had done something wrong or made mistakes. The action of documenting was therefore the best thing that I did. Without my written testimony, what I said would have been lost. Is it unusual that people are afraid of speaking out? Silence can allow scandals to brew. One teacher's remark explained the ignorance, "You should not have used his initials." Another's comment was completely out of the park, "You should never have put it in writing."

I found resources at the library and purchased books to find inspirational reading. *The Courage to Teach*[5], *Chicken Soup for the Soul*[6] and the Bible gave me words to say. I picked out a bright red dress to wear. A grandmother of one of the children, also a neighbor of mine, made me a cat vest earlier that year, which I wore over the dress.

Myth: Your voice does not matter.

After April 22, I had no intention of asking to return. I was already shark bait, and food for a barracuda. However, the message of "get out" had to be explained to the parents. By removing me, the administration had broken laws and set a dangerous precedent. With the teachers' reactions, I can guarantee you, even then, they would not speak up. It had been a heavy hand that was used against me. I expected more puzzle pieces and a window of opportunity to present my case. I had already been shown the door, but I had to be heard.

At the School Board meeting that May 18, 1998, neither the boy's parents, the Board of Education attorney nor Pipa were present. The Superintendent and Board members were seated. My husband accompanied me to this Board meeting. Many parents and colleagues showed up to give nonverbal backing or to witness what I had to say. It was the evening that two received "Teacher of the Year" awards. (Do not get me started on that tainted reward.) Obviously, I was not one.

I stood up to speak. The Superintendent did not want me to and the BOE President tried to stop me at the end of three minutes. But one parent told the Board member, "Let her talk." So, the Board allowed me to speak beyond the three-minute limit. I had written my speech in front of the Blessed Sacrament at Our Lady of Sorrows Church, a sanctuary for me. I wanted to make sure I was surrendered to God and not to any worldly ideology. I used computer paper with pictures of angels, so I could stay positive.

I addressed the parents as follows.

I am here tonight to address issues that concern the children in my class and matters of public concern. Please be aware that I am not seeking changes in my work status. However, I am requesting permission to meet with the children. On April 22, when I was told I could no longer stay in my classroom, I did not have the opportunity to say goodbye. I understand that my absence is being handled as a crisis, as though I were dead. The children need to see that I am indeed alive.

During the last few weeks, I have been relaxing, reading, reflecting, and listening. In turn, this gives me the courage to respond to the parents' concerns. Richard Reese, editor of the Catholic Digest once said, "While we were made to perfection, we were not made to achieve this perfection on our own. In fact, failure, trial and error, progress and regress, are all part of our nature as human beings. We succeed, eventually, not through individual effort alone, but with help from each other and from our creator. The only real failure is not to try, over and over."[7]

An example of a perfect assist appeared in the Catholic Digest. "It was a warm afternoon at a fast-food restaurant. We were four mothers, strangers watching our children.

Suddenly, one of the little boys banged his forehead. Immediately, his mom ran to console him. Meanwhile, one mother picked up the paper refuse, and another attended a baby that had been left alone, a fourth hurried to get ice. Then, a worker brought an ice pack. The commotion ended and we separated, each remembering the teamwork we had experienced. We had been united in our concerns for that little boy."[8]

I have taken the last few weeks to reflect on how we arrived at this point. Reading and listening to the news reminds me daily of how I got here. The prolific reports of school violence have forever changed me. Shannon Wright's name and courage are forever etched in my heart. The day she gave her life protecting her students will be one I will always honor. When rescuers are asked why they risked their lives, they often respond with "What would you have done?" Shannon Wright never had a chance to ask that question. Elie Wiesel states, "Let us not forget, there is always the moment when the moral choice is made. Often it is because of one person that we were able to make a different choice for humanity, for life. We must learn from them and in gratitude we must remember them."

Moral choices are not always made in such dramatic circumstances. Most of us have time to see the signs and act. With the ever-increasing incidence of violence in our nation's schools, we must be aware we are dealing directly with moral and life and death situations. Lawrence Kohlberg states that moral education must deal directly with action, not just reasoning. Moral dilemmas must be integrated in the curriculum. The classroom and school are community. Therefore, just as in community living, real moral issues, not just hypothetical situations, must be confronted. The Holocaust curriculum, mandated to be taught in New Jersey schools, instructs us to teach children in the K through two levels the concepts of respect and trust, and to apply concepts of respect and trust to self and others. It also states that it understands that feelings are personal, but some feelings, such as feeling sorry for people who do terribly bad things, are wrong. Feeling sorry for abuse and violence is actually enabling. Experts agree that the cycle of violence must be broken for the sake of healing.

Stephen Covey in *The Seven Habits of Highly Effective Families*[9] refers to language needing to be provocative enough to establish good habits of life. Language should reflect a focus on the things we can do something about. An anonymous writer in *Chicken Soup for the Soul*[10] remarks, "Little eyes are upon you, and they are watching day and night." As parents and teachers, we must set an example to the young.

I believe as a teacher and a parent of two children that I do set a good example, acknowledging that I am not perfect. I believe that my concerns as a parent and a teacher are valid. I followed the chain of command throughout the year regarding the concerns. Based on certain circumstances, I felt more needed to be done. The administration and the Board of Education disagreed. They felt I made a mistake. They took away my increment and gave me time out. Of the three options they gave me, I decided to use my accumulated sick days.

I would like to quote Florida Scott Maxwell (1883-1979), who stated the following. "Some uncomprehended law holds us at a point of conflict where we have no choice, where we do not like that which we love, where good and bad are inseparable partners, and impossible to tell apart, and where we, heartbroken and ecstatic, can only resolve the conflict by blindly taking it into our hearts. This used to be called being in the hands of God. Has anyone any better words to describe it?"

My association representative stated to me that the Board of Education made a mountain out of a molehill. We must now climb this mountain. In biblical terms, we have always learned something about human nature when those mountains are climbed. The message brought back from the summit always challenged us to try to do better.

My class this year was Courageous Cats, and they certainly had to be. Last year's class was The Beautiful Butterflies. In *I Never Saw Another Butterfly*,[11] a child was quoted as saying "I would like to go away alone, where there are other nicer people. Somewhere into the far unknown, where no one kills another. More of us, a thousand strong will reach that goal before too long." That child, facing the most hopeless of situations, never gave up hope. The children died in the Holocaust.

The start of my childhood school days began with Psalm 100. I would like to close with Psalm 102. "Listen to my prayers, O Lord, and hear my cry for help! When I am in trouble, do not turn away from me. Listen and answer quickly when I call. Our children will live in safety, and under your protection their descendants will be secure."

God's greatest commandment is about love. There is a childhood saying, "If a child lives with love, that child learns to love." A world without love and respect may appear to be beautiful, but it is just spiritually empty.

After I spoke, one citizen, who later became a Board member, voiced his appreciation.

While the adults in the audience remained silent, a Beautiful Butterfly, by then a third-grade student, got up to the microphone to ask the Board to allow me to say goodbye to the students. She delivered wisdom, eloquently. Her mother told me that, although she did not want to bring her daughter, the child was insistent. She was a bright, yet quiet child and special. Her comments meant the world to me and probably shocked others. Like an angel, she was delivering a clear message. Something inspired her and she, in turn, inspired me. She had more guts than all the adults put together. My Beautiful Butterfly and I used our voices at the public microphone.

The reporter who had covered the Board meeting in early May apologized for not reaching out to me. I told her she had opened a closed door.

After the meeting, my husband said he sensed evil in the cafeteria. His comment surprised me because he did not normally speak in such terms or call people evil. He indicated a woman sitting at the center of the table. The woman, to whom he referred, was the Superintendent.

On a Friday in June, a certified letter, delivered to my house, expected my presence at yet another closed-door meeting scheduled for the next Monday. Given less than a weekend to prepare, I did not have time to get legal assistance. At that point I did not want any association representative, county or local, to go with me. Returning would have been for financial reasons only, and I would have been more vulnerable to trumped up charges. How then could I turn to God and say, "Thanks for rescuing me, but I do not trust You anymore to provide. God had just taken me out of an evil situation, and I had to continue to trust Him.

I did not go to the Monday Board meeting and never did find out its purpose. That afternoon, my daughter handed me a card with a rainbow advising to trust in God. The rumor mill had it that I was going to be placed in an LRC position in addition to teaching the gifted and talented program. This rumor was surprising to learn since this would directly contradict the principal's explanation to the Board regarding my reassignment in 1996 to a regular classroom.

I did get a good kick in the ass for motivation to forge ahead through the storm. It was hard for me to distinguish among those from whom I was getting messages. It's a fine line when walking with God because at the same time, the battle rages with the devil.

The certified letter received on June 23 listed the return address of the boy's parentts. I could only guess at how they obtained mine as I was not listed in the phone book. They sent me their Notice of Tort Claim, which did not have a docket number or attorney's name. I called the representative, but he was avoiding my phone calls. I did learn that no matter what, the Board would be providing my defense in court should it get that far. I had not stepped outside my responsibilities or obligations as an employee, so they would have to represent me. The irony was clear.

At one time, the union representative said that the parents would get their "$5000 and go." An insurance settlement for having an out-of-control child could be possible if the district wanted to push the problems under the proverbial rug. When I called them for information, they would not answer any questions. Indeed, with a shooting, the cost could not have been measured in dollars and cents. People do try to seek justice through monetary settlements, and insurance companies pay out and pass the burden onto its other customers.

Crickets! I had heard nothing from the School Board, so I called the courthouse. They had no record of any Notice of Tort Claim. If it were a legal document, the parents were the aggressors. I decided I would face my adversary this time; the mother could not refuse to testify.

I ended up calling the School Board attorney, and he told me not to "lose any sleep over" it. I did lose sleep, but I have since learned that anyone can file a meritless claim or lawsuit. Did the district pay out money to the parents as my Association representative predicted? He said, "They would get their $5,000 and go."

One set of attorneys I called, as recommended by a former colleague, had been contacted by another party. They already knew of me. Without stating this, I deduced the parents had contacted this attorney. The firm was not listed on the Notice of Tort Claim. In my consults, attorneys said their case had less hope than mine to be heard. But it motivated me to do research and correspond to various parties to obtain information and assistance. The parents had a problem with the First Amendment also.

After contacting the First Amendment Center at Vanderbilt University in 1998, I received a response from the analyst who consulted with an attorney about employee speech. I received, on October 29, the reply from the analyst on the First Amendment Rights of teachers.

The U.S. Supreme Court wrote in the Tinker case that "Neither students nor teachers shed their constitutional rights to freedom of speech and expression at the schoolhouse gate." Of course, schoolteachers are public employees. Therefore, their First Amendment rights are analyzed under the traditional public employee speech cases. The initial question is whether the speech constitutes or touches upon a matter of public concern or is it only a private matter. If the speech is a matter of public concern, then courts ask whether the employee's interest in expressing herself outweighs the efficiency interests of the employer.

Sincerely, JF Religious Freedom Analyst

In the April 26 bulletin from St. Catherine of Sienna Church in Sea Girt, NJ, under the title, *Food for Thought* was an explanation of Gospel values:

The Apostles would have applauded the concept of our First Amendment right to free speech. When the authorities tried to make them stop talking about Jesus and spreading His message, the apostles refused, even though their act put them in danger of suffering the same fate as He did. Today, we probably won't put ourselves in danger of death if we bring issues of justice or compassion into work-place decision making, but we may open ourselves to being ostracized. Ask for the grace to make Jesus' values truly a part of both your public and private life.

You can get encouragement in church bulletins!

If He can hold the world, He can hold this moment and me.

WHAT YOU DO NOT KNOW
COULD HURT YOU

I taught in a small district and was assigned to a small building. Many people like large campuses, but I liked the intimacy of teaching in a small school where I could have contact with most students. However, while the teachers' experiences taught them what a child was like, it did not necessarily tell them what to do.

Beginning while the boy in question was in kindergarten, the staff had witnessed his aggressive physical outbursts towards other children. While on playground duty, I had witnessed him repeatedly kicking a boy, identified as his friend, while the child was down on the ground. I reported the incident. His kindergarten teacher was relieved that someone else besides her had documented the behavior. In his first-grade year, after many physical assaults on other children, a formal assessment took place assigning him to homebound instruction for three months. After an evaluation process, the child returned with a personal aide and assistance from the learning resource room teacher, while the other first grade teacher took over the instruction. He was prescribed medicine for attention deficits, and his aggressive outbursts were monitored through counseling and behavior modification techniques. Private family counseling had also been recommended.

Upon entering his second-grade year, the intervention procedures that had been established the preceding year were discontinued. Little was shared with me formally, but the informal discussions together with my experience were valuable. I adapted the curriculum and routines to accommodate him. But, overall, it was not enough for him. He still exhibited aggression towards other children, and defiant behavior towards the staff.

We started the year 1998 with no personal aide, no medication, and no follow-up counseling. Resource room instruction provided individual attention throughout the day. However, the child worked in a setting of twenty-four other children, with marginal support, despite many academic and social problems.

I relied on the learning resource room teacher and her aide, who were both familiar with the child from his first-grade year. Certain behavioral signs noted by the resource room teacher indicated an increase in aggression, and the LRC teacher identified trigger situations, which helped us mitigate outbursts. We adjusted activities where the child had difficulty in first grade in order to accommodate his needs in my class. We made adaptations to seating arrangements and schedules to minimize negative verbal or physical reactions. Although tapping of a pencil did not disturb me, the LRC teacher advised that the pencil tap indicated frustration. Although I had worked with at-risk students and children who exhibited poor behavior or lacked coping skills, this child demonstrated behaviors that exceeded the norm.

Even on the first day, the child entered several minutes after the other children with his mother. As he came in, he stood surveying the class. That was noteworthy. All the children had either been in his kindergarten or first grade programs. With much prompting, his mother left, and he took his seat.

Later that year we no longer entered and exited through our individual classroom doors. All the children entered from the playground through the main back door. We could only surmise that the change in procedure was probably implemented as a safety measure. The building was for sale and one day in the summer, I had questioned the presence of a businessman. No one was supposed to tour the building without an escort. Pipa did support me then when I escorted him to the office.

Most teachers can attest to a honeymoon phase, where everyone is on his or her best behavior, both students and staff. A strong sense of welcoming is usually present. That year was no different. For the first two weeks, with the benefit of a behavior modification chart from his first grade, a reward system and constant supervision, he experienced success.

In addition, the psychologist developed a rewards system of points, charted multiple times daily. The standards set were based on acceptable school behavior. Acceptable or outstanding behaviors were awarded a score of 1 or 2. Inappropriate behaviors received a 0. While the guideline to follow the scoring was subjective, we determined that, if within the same time period he acted inappropriately but was able to regain his composure, he scored a 1. A list of rewards and consequences was listed to reinforce acceptable actions and lessen the inappropriate ones. The psychologist rewarded him based on his weekly scores, which were given in addition to the classroom rewards for individual and group efforts. Positive reinforcement and praise, the primary means used to improve behavior for all the children, proved to be successful on good days. We used timeout for inappropriate behaviors.

The honeymoon did not last long. After a two-day absence, he started refusing to complete or participate in activities he did not want to, or which would frustrate him. At the same time, I had to maintain academics and reinforcement for the other students. It was certainly a change from my Beautiful Butterfly year. We adjusted game days, pajama day, free activities and some rewards but not all triggers were predictable,

Legally, all staff working with the child were to be informed of pertinent data regarding this educational plan. However, the Child Study Team did not share everything with me as a classroom teacher and shared even less with the special area teachers. The CST met once a year to discuss the classified students but details in individual education plans were not shared, as they should have been. I had dual certification—IEP was part of my vocabulary—neither was it a foreign term for any teacher.

Coming back to what was stated in my hearing about special area teachers and what they can learn about students, all special area teachers were invited to a meeting to discuss the special needs students in "Re: Special Education Articulation Meeting: Thank you for taking the time to get acquainted with the special needs students in our program." It should be noted that the other second grade teacher's name was not on the memo because she did not have the classified children on her roll.

Duty schedules warranted that the aide in the cafeteria, the one who was the education aide for the LRC, record her observations at lunchtime. She was a neighbor to the student and had a loving grandmotherly attitude to all the children. This meant that, although she meant well, she did not like to report unsatisfactory behaviors. I therefore could not count on her accuracy. She should have been in on meetings also as well as directed to complete the chart.

Her attitude was consistent with volunteers. One day, in the new cafeteria, which was larger and held more classes than the old school, I had a conversation with a volunteer about documenting behaviors. She said she did not want repercussions on her child, so she was afraid to report them. In this situation, my student was not the culprit.

By design, lunch and recess are not as structured and there is less individual supervision. Triggering situations could therefore go unnoticed, but scoring during these times was required and important. It was noted that this child did not like to lose. In recess or in physical education class, if his team was losing, he had a hard time dealing effectively. He would argue his point of view, very often ending in getting a 0 for that time increment. Depending on the behavior, timeout would be a crucial step.

I had found that by the end of September 1997, the chart utilizing time increments did not reflect our schedules. It may have worked in his first grade, but we in second grade had different teaching styles. Our small or large groups were often longer because we incorporated the whole language model of teaching. Therefore, we readjusted the targeting timeframe for reporting behavior to 30-minute increments to give a greater chance of receiving positive results. In addition, I placed tangible signs on his desk to identify positive or negative behavior such as a happy face and a frowning face with a short list of acceptable and unacceptable behaviors.

This child was bright; he could read quite well. Providing him with the same courtesy as the other students, I used the three strikes rule: two warnings before a 0. Socially unacceptable behavior, in any social setting, was assigned as a strikeout. Examples were hitting another student, taking something that did not belong to them, or calling names. Bullying was not a general term frequently used then but, if a child were inappropriate, some behaviors could fall into that category. Any behavior that jeopardized his safety or the safety of others scored a 0, with intervention sought.

The child took home the chart daily to be signed and returned. I am not sure whether the charts demonstrated the best plan of action, but it was something agreed upon by the team and the parents. The parents may have considered the charts as punishment. I can understand that strain. All the same, they had constant information of positive and negative behaviors. We were not certain as to how the charts were being used at home. On his part, the child had a hard time understanding how someone could contribute to class rewards, and questioned when he earned a petal colored in a group reward flower.

In October 1997, the LRC teacher and I had requested a group meeting with the parents, CST, and the principal. Pipa included the child in this meeting. His behavior was inappropriate, as one may guess. A few team members laughed as though his reactions were funny. It was clear the child was too young to be in the discussion as his behaviors clearly reflected.

After Pipa decided to take him back to the class, I accompanied her with the child to his regularly scheduled activity so the adults could meet. As she tried to put her arm around him, he pulled away so roughly his jacket sleeve came off his arm. The meeting was not successful other than convincing the parents to try the medication once again. Since it was prescribed, the team suggested, for consistency, to maintain the medication schedule. Rightfully, the parents questioned the medication. In the last 25 years, red flags have been raised about the side effects of ADHD medications and there are more medication options today.

Please note: because teachers have been criticized for wanting students on medication and sometimes blamed for over prescribing, teachers and CST are not medical prescribers. Medication is an option for certain diagnoses, but a medically trained professional must prescribe.

This was the first formal meeting. We were hoping to coordinate efforts with the home. It was evident that the parents did not agree with us or with each other for that matter, as to which path to take to help the child. But we were dealing with physically violent and/or verbal outbursts and had to do something. All children have a right to be educated in a safe environment. It is not a new concept. New Jersey law demanded it. However, securing those rights for the children and staff was a constant struggle.

The Child Study Team Director had questioned my request for the child to be sent home one day in the fall. It had been a trying day from the start because of an incident reported by the teacher on morning playground duty. My documentation of concerns goes as follows:

November 3, 1997
Dear Mrs. Principal,
Thank you for supporting my request today to have the child removed from the classroom and sent home. My decision to make such a request was based on the decision-making process that took place in the meeting with the child's parents on 10/30/1997. It was decided that, if the child exhibited unsafe behavior towards himself or another person, he was to be removed from the situation and, if necessary, sent home. In my professional judgment, the child's behavior on the playground and then in the classroom on 11/3/1997 warranted the need to send the child home.
It has been brought to my attention, by the LRC teacher, Mrs. K, that a Child Study Team member has some concern

about the request to send the child home because he did not actually hit another child in the afternoon altercation, as he did on the playground before school began. It is in response to this that I'm writing this documentation. I am concerned that the interpretation of unsafe behavior has been distorted. The child should not reach the stage of hitting another child before he can be removed from the classroom. If that is the case, the child was given the opportunity to improve his behavior by remaining in class after he hit another child before the 8:30 a.m. bell. Miss G, the teacher on morning duty, had documented the incident. The child did not calm down after the second incident. He continued to exhibit defiant behavior, scribbled on his desk, refused to complete assignments, and refused to go with the LRC teacher and the nurse. In addition, per the joint conference on 10/30/1997, the child is not excluded from the disciplinary procedures.

Board policy 5180 requires each student to adhere to the rules and regulations. The handbook for teachers, last dated 1995-1996, states the primary responsibility for discipline rests with the classroom teacher. Following the guidelines set forth in the meeting and in written policy, there should not be further debate as to the outcomes resulting from the child's unsafe behavior exhibited on the playground, nor in the classroom. As we mentioned briefly at the end of the day 11/3/1997, we will need to brainstorm other avenues related to the child's behavior. The behaviors the child exhibited today, in relation to peer interaction, occurred even though he had earned 2s in most of the areas of teacher-directed activities. Thank you for your help in this situation.

I received a copy back from the Principal with a note jotted at the top:

MC, I am confident and comfortable with my decision to uphold your request based on his behavior. [Principal's initials]

We had to get the principal involved because the administrator is the only one legally able to send a child home. The teacher can only recommend. On this day, I did receive back up. I also had copied the local association President, but no mention was made of plans that would deny him hope for his future. I was not reprimanded for including the eighth-grade teacher on this documentation.

There were a few other times when Pipa did confirm my apprehensions about where the behavior patterns were leading. One female student started becoming fearful, and her mother approached me about the headaches and stomachaches that showed her reluctance to come to school. I questioned what it was I was doing to cause this, but the mother did not think it was my actions or inactions. Lunchtime was particularly a problem if she made it to school at all. I asked the aide if she had noticed any-thing in the lunchroom. It turned out the girl sat across from the student in the cafeteria and was seated near him in class. Children have assigned seats in the cafeteria as well. The little girl was a caring and kind child, so the placement was not random. The girl was smart, but sensitive. She had been in his previous year's class and became frightened by the continued stress of having the boy near her. This was documented in December 1997. Pipa assured the girl that no one was to harm another and she spoke with the boy. We made alternate seating arrangements and kept them separated as much as possible.

Heading into late December through January 1998, there con-tinued to be fewer scores of 2. Even though our expectations for improvement in conduct grew, his conduct began to deteriorate. Holidays always play a role in children's mannerisms, so we attributed the downward trend to the season.

His records throughout the late fall and early winter showed fluctuating scores. The school's small population and a true atmo-sphere of caring enabled us to keep behaviors under control. As directed, timeout enabled my students, myself, and the child to regroup.

Once that year I was called to serve jury duty. I had to serve over two days. I left detailed notes for the substitute. I came into school as soon as I could daily. I was selected for questioning for one trial but was honest and told the lawyers and judge I was concerned about my class. They dismissed me. The substitute did leave me a lengthy note about the child with her concerns. She thought he needed hugs. How many substitutes had training twenty-five years ago? How many substitutes are trained today? They may have to rely on gut reactions.

On one occasion, the CST members praised me because, after one of his outbursts, I had the presence of mind to leave and take the children to the library. The nurse came to assist on that day. There were rumors, per the nurse, that the family may have wanted to move to a larger township but working in a much larger school with new people would be challenging for him.

Child Study Team members knew this boy for three years and more history than I did about his adverse reactions, but they did not work their magic in a classroom setting. CST members administer tests, interview, and work one-on-one with these students, intent on saving one starfish at a time. I had 25.

At the April 20, 1998, hearing, the attorney questioned my authority to label the family as distressed, it's true I did not have a medical degree. But I did have educational skills and eyes to see. Were they questioning why he came in with a black eye one day while I was still teaching him, and his explanation related to hockey? In 2002, I learned that the child allegedly had found his brother dead of a drug overdose. When I obtained this information about the boy years later, it was not I who reached out; people came to me. His full name, not just his initials, was starting to appear in the police blotter for assaults and warrants as he got older. There were at least two high schools. The parents and the school district had failed him as a young child. Did they recollect my words?

A New York City teacher sued the New York City school system because of violent outbursts by a first grader. People may scoff, but first graders can be very violent. Give them access to weapons and wait if you dare. The suit claimed that the school district knew about the child's violent tendencies yet failed to notify or prepare the teachers. Teachers have the right to be safe, but physically controlling a violent child can often lead to retribution. The New York teacher was put in a difficult situation.

In January 2023, a first-grade child shot his teacher in a school in Virginia. She survived. Interviewed on network news, she explained that she would never forget the look on the child's face as he pulled the trigger. She is suing her district because warning signs were missed, although there was prior knowledge. The mother of the boy has received jail time related to the shooting.

CHAPTER 9

YOU KNOW THE DRILLS

Our little building was old and required major repair work. It also was in a prime real estate location. The voters had passed a referendum two years earlier to build a new Community School that would house kindergarten through eighth grade, thus consolidating the four elementary schools into one large campus. The new school was partially ready for occupancy in December 1997.

The BOE decided, before the start of the 97-98 year that students from the two primary schools housing third through eighth graders, would move over the Christmas break, although construction was not complete. The two other schools would begin the 1998-99 year in the new building. In a staff meeting, we were all given keys to the new classrooms that we chose in order of seniority. We ignored that warning sign and ploy by the administration. So, we decorated for the next year, we brought supplies to our classrooms for the next year, because we had an open house for the next school year. I named my next year's class, Carlino's Kind Kids.

We experienced unexplained problems with the fire alarm system, especially after the Christmas break, in our little school. I was assured that it was not my student pulling the alarms, but my first reaction was, "Was it a child?" Evacuated to the playground, the fire department and police came to investigate. Every teacher is used to handling disruptions as small costs to pay until they are not. When drills become regular, something is not normal.

One day, we had to retreat to the playground for a lengthy time because the fluorescent light blew out in a closet. The odor created was irritating and spread throughout the one-story building. The smell reminded me of a stink bomb, but I was assured that the smell was from the busted bulb. Several more days throughout the month of January, alarms were sounded that sent us to the playground to wait.

On February 5, we had to evacuate once again. The unusual timing of this alarm was that it sounded first at the firehouse, before going off at the school. The janitor came and told us verbally to exit. Connecting dots, suspicious minds turned to administration's motivations. It was believed there might have been competition between the two people who were to be Co-Principals. Several of us thought that our leader was threatened by the fact that she was not in the new building to take control. I told the LRC teacher that morning, "Someone was trying to get us out." By 1:00 p.m. that afternoon, sure enough, administration announced that the school was not safe, and it was being shut down.

The parents were called, and the children sent home, while the teachers had to stay to prepare. We had four days to pack up our belongings, move them and be ready for class on the following Tuesday. Parents volunteered to pack. I openly discussed my feelings. They were not thrilled either, but they chose to believe when told the building was unsafe. It was a violation of our contract to force us to work the weekend, so I did not work. With doubts that this was legitimate, I told two other staff members my suspicions, and put in writing to Pipa, asking about the motivation for the rapid decision and to reconsider it. To be honest, I would have worked 24 hours a day as I had done in the past if I believed the fire story. The district provided some transporting of supplies, but we mostly drove our materials in our personal cars. County Day workers were used, which may have been a violation of law since day workers were from the County jail. I was ready for class on that Tuesday.

Do I sound like a whiner? As a building representative, with gut feelings and no legal background, I still asked questions. I received an invite to discuss my handwritten note and was verbally reprimanded. In our little chat, Pipa snidely referenced my editorial about abortion which had recently been published, advising I should write a formal one about the move; but my little note was not editorial worthy. However, the note did create a spark. Moving boxes late on the Friday night, I saw the Superintendent watching me carry them in, while she was on the phone with someone. The Superintendent would not have been able to accuse me of not doing my job despite how I felt about the motivation for the move.

Teachers who had moved in December were already experiencing problems that disrupted the regular routines. In good spirit, we all pitched in together and bought donuts, bagels, and coffee for them. When I delivered the breakfast treats to the middle school teachers on behalf of my school, this gave me an opportunity to see a few teachers. They made lists of incomplete work. The new rooms were sizably smaller as well, and the storage limited.

I was able to finish the task of moving most items and setting up the new room, working diligently on Thursday, Friday and Monday. Long hours, no lunch and no chit-chat worked for me. I did not work on that Saturday or Sunday for contractual reasons. Others did; they did not directly question the judgments of administrators, while grumbling amongst themselves. We should have all set up a grievance procedure, but most teachers will not question the administration even when they blatantly lie. Lack of safety did not keep us from going back in to finish packing and moving our supplies over several weeks.

I recognized that a rapid change in routine would not be good for the kids either. Children, who used to walk to the previous elementary school without crossing major streets and intersections, now had to cross a main thoroughfare, in a flood zone. Parents had to drive. The parking and traffic were horrendous with cars exiting onto the busiest street in the area. Plus, the building was still under construction. The Superintendent had to mop a very wet atrium floor on very rainy days.

A fire at the one remaining school building broke out forcing them to take up early residence. Why should they have been left

CHAPTER 9

out? Two fires in two schools—would you be suspicious? The new building took in all the students six months earlier than first announced. No schedules remained the same. The cafeteria was very loud and the teachers' room very tiny. Our enrichment activities took a hit as well. In the smaller room, and a building not quite right, we were discouraged to do "Cooking with Mrs. K" because fire safety and setting off alarms, of all things, mattered. So, we tried to use the home economics room. This caused sparks to fly, but not due to tangible flames, when the Home Economics teacher threatened to grieve anyone using the room because her job was cut to part time. I respected her and refused to use her room.

The technology experts instructed us to place our desks under the new computer stands. I suggested to the teachers not to sit under the fixtures. Looking at the brackets in the ceiling, I recalled that the computer monitor gave way in a kindergarten class in my children's school. That one had fallen out of cinder block walls. Contractors used drywall. I did not trust the structure's integrity. Weeks after I left, the unit in my former classroom did fall out, according to the janitor, who was my friend. Why do we have premonitions?

Not one word was mentioned in the closed-door hearing about me questioning the move or the construction. Why not? One of the three schools was razed, and new houses built. The other K-2 building, which also had a fire, was rented to a private school and used for years.

WHAT WOULD
THE PARENTS THINK?

There were many times I saw parents and students and explained, when they asked me to come back, that I could not. Just as God can turn around what is meant for evil, for good, people can use what is meant for good for evil purposes. Could my situation have been designed to be a distraction to the parents so they would not learn what was going on in the district and the new school?

I did not have one other parent ever threaten to sue me. On the contrary, they informed administration of their dissatisfaction. When do you think these letters should have been sent to the school and to me, before or after March 24? Their sentiment, besides affirming me, meant that they had insights of which I knew nothing concrete. The child was hurting their children, and the parents knew it. I did not have these letters in May, although the parents requested that I receive them. Could the correspondence be used in a court of law if they used no names?

Petition: [Signed by twelve parents]
We, the undersigned, strongly believe that our children's safety is being jeopardized by being in the same classroom with a specific classmate. His most recent display of negative aggressive behavior was on April 27, 1998, which resulted in his suspension for two days. This is not an isolated incident but one of several reported incidents. This constant exposure to this type of behavior is having a negative impact on our children. We

believe that our children's safety and education is a priority. Can you guarantee that our children will be in an environment that is safe and conducive to learning if this child remains in this classroom? The PHILOSOPHY OF EDUCATION of the public school district states: "We believe the school system is responsible for creating an environment for learning." We are requesting you, as members of the Board of Education, to carefully consider our concerns and determine if this type of environment is being provided for our children.

On April 30, 1998, I received a copy of this letter with the cover note, "Mrs. Carlino, we have been asked to send this to you."

Dear Members of the Board,
I am writing this letter as a concerned parent of a second-grade student of Mrs. B's (and Mrs. Carlino's former second-grade class.) An incident occurred during the lunch period in the cafeteria where my son was kicked by a fellow student. Although he was not seriously injured, he was mentally upset by this incident. After speaking to the Principal, I was advised that this student was suspended. I have heard many stories concerning the student, but I feel it is only fair to comment on the incidents which directly involved my son. This boy in the past has bullied my son and last year on the day when he was removed from his first-grade class and transferred into my son's class, my son was afraid to go to school. I walked with him every day and stayed in the school yard until the bell rang, as I still do, so as to make sure there would be no incidents involving this boy and my son.

I attended the meeting last week which the Principal arranged to try to clear up questions parents have involving Mrs. Carlino's removal from the class. Although I was appreciative of the school's concern to have this meeting, I was left with unresolved questions and concerns about the actual reason Mrs. Carlino was removed as my son's teacher. I was very distraught when I learned that her removal had been caused by some incident which concerned this boy and his family. While I understand that there are delicate issues which cannot be discussed due to legal reasons, I still do not understand why the teacher, who deeply cares about her students and their families, would be the subject of this type of treatment. My husband and I are very upset with the removal of Mrs. Carlino as our son's teacher. We have the greatest respect for Mrs. Carlino and see the wonderful things she has done for our son. We truly believe that it is because of her that our son enjoys school so much. She has worked very hard with us to improve his self-esteem and help him overcome his shyness. His reading and spelling are better than ever, and his grades reflect this improvement. Please be advised I do not have any negative concerns about the replacement teacher. From what I have seen and heard, she is a wonderful replacement.

I would, however, ask the Board to reexamine the situation involving Mrs. Carlino and reinstate her to a position. Our children miss her and so do we. I have firsthand experience with her and know that she is a caring person and teacher. This district and our children will suffer with the loss of such a wonderful teacher. It would be a disgrace if her concerns and possible foresight into a problem were swept under the carpet and future incidents involving the student occur.

Very truly yours, [Signed by a parent]

I was fully aware the mother stayed until the children entered the building, but not the reason. I also received the copy of a letter from the parents of one of my Beautiful Butterflies.

Dear Superintendent,

We are writing to you today to express our concern regarding the removal of Mrs. Carlino from her classroom. We have found Mrs. Carlino to be a very caring teacher. She extends herself well beyond what one would expect from a classroom teacher.

Our child, who was in her second-grade class last year, benefited greatly, not only intellectually, but socially as well. Showing an example of how Mrs. Carlino extends herself beyond what one would expect, we would like to relate a story from last year.

The children in their class were involved with raising butterflies; in fact, they were nicknamed The Beautiful Butterflies. They were anxiously awaiting the hatching from the cocoons, but time ran out on the school year. Mrs. Carlino, on her own time, called every child and arranged a convenient time to meet and release the butterflies. In addition, she had gift bags for all the children who showed up. It saddens us to think that our school system may lose a caring and dedicated teacher like Mrs. Carlino. She is a person who truly cares for her students. It is our hope that you and the Board of Education will reconsider the decision to move her from her classroom.

Sincerely, [Signed by both parents]

I received a handwritten note and Pipa received a typed one, copied to me by the same parent. In her letter to the Principal, the parent was very complimentary about how Pipa handled the meeting on April 24. However, the date shows April 23. Surreal situations sometimes confuse us.

I attended the meeting held this morning on behalf of the parents of the children who were students in Mrs. Carlino's classroom. The events over the past three days seem very surrealistic to me as a parent. I can only imagine what it has been like for you. I wanted to write and thank you for your kindness, compassion, and most of all bravery for standing before a group of parents who were less than happy, to say the least. I understand the difficult position you were in with regard to confidentiality since I am a (job listed). I feel you did a remarkable job. You withstood every criticism, every dissatisfied word, every murmur, every grumble, and you did it with poise and a great deal of humility. And once the School Board attorney left to go to court, you did it alone. I cannot think of any other individual who would have withstood that kind of pressure with the same amount of grace.

I have every confidence in the new teacher and every bit of confidence in the staff at the school. This has been a very unique and difficult situation. There is always going to be a person in the crowd who will be dissatisfied about how a situation is handled. Nonetheless, it is water under the bridge, and we need to move forward. And we know that in all things, God works for the good of those who love him who have been called according to His purpose - Romans 8:28. One of my favorite authors, Anne Anderson, has a unique interpretation in the above verse. It means, God never takes away except to give us back something better. It means we must be brave enough and determined enough to wait because often God takes time to turn a painful situation to good.

It means we can embrace our pain and not resent it because the blessing is coming.

Now, the handwritten letter dated April 26, 1998, directed to me.

Words cannot express how sorry we are about all that has happened this past week, and truth be told, we have no idea what happened! All I can tell you is that you are and will remain, in our thoughts and prayers during this troubled time. I am sure you have gone through an awful lot as well. I wanted to share one of my favorite Bible verses which I feel is appropriate all the way around.

And we know that in all things, God works for the good of those who love him, who have been called according to His purpose - Romans 8:28. My favorite author, Ann Anderson, who follows up with this says it means God never takes away except to give us back something better. It means we must be brave enough and determined enough to wait, because it often takes God time to turn a painful situation to good. It means we can embrace our pain and not resent it because the blessing is coming. God bless and restore peace in your life. Hope to see you again; you will be missed.

I did not know what to think other than the fact the woman spoke out of both sides of her mouth because of her job. Throughout the years I have appreciated the mood captured in the meeting on April 24. Years later, we took intensive Bible Study classes together. She had changed careers and had experienced some hardships herself. We truly appreciated each other and our experiences. The Scripture chosen is so very true. God does indeed work all things meant for evil for good for those who love Him.

Here is a copy of another letter written to the Board by a concerned parent.

April 28, 1998
Dear Superintendent, Board of Education, and the Principal,

It is with deep concern that I write to you today. I would like to inform you of a situation in the lunchroom between my child and the troubled boy. Last week he was sitting next to my child at lunch and proceeded to spray milk from his mouth through a straw. My child came home with dried milk in her hair and on her clothes. I asked if she had told anyone about the incident. She said she was afraid to tell. This is not the first time this boy has bullied my child. Last year in his first-grade class he sat across from her in their block of desks and continuously kicked her in the shins. It escalated to a point where we requested her seat to be moved. I am now requesting that my daughter not be placed in his class next year as her happiness and safety are my first concern. His outrageous behavior and his unwillingness to conform to class rules interrupt the teaching and educational process of every child in his class. He has been and continues to be a daily distraction. It is with regret that I am requesting this, but I feel I have no other recourse. Please place a copy of this letter in my child's file and also one in the young boy's file.

Thank you. [Written by the girl's mother]

I received a note on or about March 26 in response to an incident with the child on March 25, the day after the disagreement with the principal. Do you think any parent would approve of what Pipa advised about child witness reports? Pipa did not want the children to speak up or a teacher to discern. In large, cursive writing I received the following:

In addition, Mrs. Carlino took the word of another child who Mrs. Carlino referred to as a neutral child. I explained to Mrs. Carlino that if there is an altercation between two children, then both children's parents are contacted stating that a few children stated that so and so did it. But a teacher should not assess that a child is neutral. Unfortunately, children jump to conclusions just like adults can.

Myth: Children do not have the right to defend themselves.

This is a different type of parent letter to compare and contrast. What kind of parent letter would be preferable?

In the book *If I Don't Make it, I Love You Survivors in the Aftermath of School Shooting*[12] the author explains failures. The chapters examine different school shootings from 2018 Santa Fe High School back to the University of Austin in 1966. In the chapter outline there is no reference to the elementary school in Jonesboro though.

February 14, 2018: Marjorie Stoneman Douglas High School: Mitchell Dworet, parent of a student killed.

It's devastating what happened to us, what happened to Nick and in relation to being a parent. I'm right here at Nick's empty bedroom. I'm here. This is where he is or was. To look at this, it's surreal still. I talk to people, I'm talking to you, sometimes it's third person for me because I can't believe that this happened. How could this happen, right?

February 2008: Northern University of Illinois: Joseph Dubowski, parent of 21-year-old Gayle.

On February 14, 2008, at around 10:40 p.m. someone effectively held my script in front of my face and lit it with a match. They told us, Laura my wife, Ryan our son and about a dozen friends, who had met us at Kishwaukee Hospital that night, that a girl matching our daughter's description had died after being airlifted to a hospital near Rockford IL. Our 21-year-old daughter, Gayle, who was a sophomore in college, was dead from a gunshot wound from the shooting that had taken place at NIU that afternoon. Suddenly everything I thought I knew about my life felt like it went up in smoke.

April 16, 2007: Margaret Herbstritt, mother of Jeremy, who died at Virginia Tech wrote ... Forever, when I hear footsteps, when I see a red Jeep, when I see a cardinal, I think of Jeremy."

In chapter 18, Gregory Gibson's son Galen Gibson died in a shooting at a college campus in 1992.

Our waking nightmare became common knowledge, an absurd violation, and an inescapable fact. Galen was dead ... At about 10:15 on the evening of Monday, December 14, 1992, he began walking through the campus, shooting people ... Then somehow he surrendered and was arrested, unharmed. His name was Wayne Lo. He had emigrated from Taiwan, China six years before ... he was wearing a sweatshirt on which was printed the motto, "Sick of it all."

Chapter 19: On November 1, 1991, a shooting spree at the University of Iowa was carried out by a man from China and not a U.S. citizen. He made a list of those he planned to kill. The victims were all adults who worked at the University.

Chapter 20: The teacher of a second-grade class recalls the children killed on the playground on January 17, 1989. It is interesting her use of the word "ordinary." Ordinary or normal, nothing stands out until it does. Gunshots changed her ordinary day.

Julia Schardt in her essay, *The Red Shoes*, redefines "ordinary:"
Ordinary because the routine of teaching can make some minutes ordinary ... Then it became extraordinary because the sound breaking the silence was not firecrackers. It was gunshots. Distant but loud, sharp, shredding the peace of my classroom.

WHAT WOULD THE PARENTS THINK?

People profile by color and race. Angry white boys in suburbs and gang members in cities are assumed to be the killers. We wonder why, when the shooter's race or sex does not fit media expectations that the headline reads differently.

Myth: School shooters are always male white supremacists.

CHAPTER 11

SEEKING LEGAL EAGLES, CHANNELING PING

On May 14, 1998, I sent a formal request via certified mail to the school district, requesting the tapes and transcripts of the closed-door hearing of April 20, 1998. I was still confused about where I was to be going. Unanswered, I waited. My request was not on the agenda on May 18, although it listed one request from the parents for the minutes.

I contacted a private attorney to represent me. An association attorney's name was given to me, but I was hesitant about contacting him. It's important for general membership to know, though it did not sink into my brain then, that dealing with my case meant showing up other members such as the Child Study Team and other teachers to be wrong. The Bible is clear about settling matters out of court. I knew enough that suing the school district meant suing the very people I wanted to protect. Moreover, taxpayers would be paying. I was not interested in suing anyone; I just wanted legal advice. My argument was with Pipa, the Superintendent, and the Board.

I thought I could get through to the association that I did not want my job back, but I did want my voice heard. I can still picture walking in the school hallway with the local association President on one of the days. He accompanied me to the meetings with the Superintendent in April. As we parted ways and I opened my classroom door, he told me I would be in a civil case. I said I would be a thorn in their sides. Turns out, a thorny dispute ensued, and my rose-colored glasses took a beating. He sat near me for the School Board hearing that May 18, 1998.

I had set up a meeting with a private attorney in early May. That same dark uncomfortable feeling that I had on the rainy night in January came over me as I waited in the reception area. We had used this attorney's services for our wills and for the purchase of our home. His partner's name gave me an eerie feeling because it was familiar. I then remembered seeing her at a meeting earlier in the year. She had been very friendly with the Principal although her husband was in a disagreement with the BOE and Superintendent. He had spoken at a Board meeting. He was not the only business administrator to have problems with the Superintendent. Two business administrators were let go under the Superintendent's leadership. Two dismissals were noteworthy in how they were treated; one was locked out of his office, and I am not sure why the business administrator of record in my closed-door hearing left the district.

I asked the attorney if he had any ties to my former employer. He said he did not, but he did work for public entities, as I later learned. He told me that I should never have gone to the closed-door meeting without an attorney present. He stated that if I were to pursue any legal action, I would have to destroy the child's family. Besides, any action would be very expensive and difficult to win because most school board decisions are upheld. He pointed out I had disagreed with the Principal but, on the other hand, the 1982 School Safety law was clear although experts seemed unaware of its implications and requirements.

In terms of destroying the boy's family, that was not my intent. I did not agree with them, but I was trying to improve our efforts. When suing a public entity, there is a limited timeframe in which you can file a Notice of Tort claim. The School Board represents the community. They lied, the community was victimized and as was pointed out to me, they had no problem with trying to destroy my family.

It was too late to voice my grievance over the Board's vote to the Commissioner's Office, the Union representative advised me.

I had missed valuable time to clear my name. Some of that missed time was because I was not sure what to do as I worked my way through so many issues, and not having the financial freedom to hire an attorney. I continued to wait and pray for clear guidance.

I then received the name of a northern N.J. law firm, who were not able to advise because they had already been contacted by an interested party.

The example of Ping was not lost on me. I needed to rely on perseverance to handle sharks, barracudas, Jezebel, court jesters and, of course, Pipa. Prayers for a wise, earthly emperor did not cause one to materialize. Each step was just like solving a puzzle.

The public meeting minutes were mailed late in June. I had not asked for them because I wanted the sworn minutes.

The teachers' associations are there to defend teachers when they are accused, whether guilty or not. We would receive cards with legal contact information in case anyone was accused of abuse. I had such mixed emotions and reactions in 1998 that I missed some opportunities that would have been legally timely.

After receiving the Notice of Tort Claim, I decided to do more research and became determined to secure the tapes/sworn testimony. But I was being denied access to them, receiving a great deal of run-around. The local association president once again agreed to accompany me to the Superintendent's office to get the minutes and the tapes. They only had the tapes. I had misgivings about taking them because I did not think they were real. If the tapes were fake, it would have been their word against mine. I was asked that day if I wanted to meet with the CST but declined.

I finally secured an attorney from the association. I had to put some level of trust into the lawyers who worked with them. In August, the attorney gave me instructions over the phone as to what to do to secure the minutes because he said that the school district hired a local service to legally transcribe the tapes. However, the district had made it extremely difficult even on the day to pick them up. Luckily, I received a phone call from the service that I could pick them up. I paid a fee for the original and copy. The cost was $630, a costly sum for someone not working, but I wrote out a check. Then the Superintendent's secretary as well as the transcriptionist's officer manager left voicemails to say I was not entitled to the copy, and I must return both copies. I saved the voicemails and called the association attorney. He stated that as long as I had paid the fees, I was entitled to both. Why did they print two? The following day when I called the staff, they admitted they were wrong in calling me to tell me I had to return one copy. They had no legal right to call me nor were they correct. Was the School Board giving those minutes to someone else?

Disturbed by my acquisition, the representative inquired as to what I planned to do with the minutes. I was not sure, but the minutes held answers to my many questions. He responded to me in writing on September 22, 1998.

Pursuant to your request, I am responding to you in writing. Last April, the Board of Education voted to withhold your increment. This decision was based on a rather lengthy non adversarial hearing and the recommendation of the Superintendent. In my opinion, the reason for the Board's action was performance related and, therefore, not subject to the grievance procedure.

The option of petitioning the Commissioner of Education was available but, as I explained to you, case law is horrendous on increment withholding petitions. The overriding response from the Department of Education is that they will not impose their judgment over the local boards.

Recognizing that you were not satisfied with the situation, I had the association approve a consultation with S.E Esquire so that you could meet and confer with an attorney at no cost to you. You did not follow up on this option.

Sometime earlier this summer you decided to seek a copy of the transcript from the hearing. At that point you began calling different employees of the association, and as a result a second consultation was approved in enabling you to meet and seek the opinion of N.R. Esquire.

You informed me in August that you were not returning to the district. I advised you to authorize me to negotiate an exit deal on your behalf. You decided to forgo any negotiations and resigned.

Now you're purchasing a copy of the transcript and seeking legal assistance from the association, and I do not know what the association can accomplish on your behalf regarding your increment or position. If you were considering civil action (offensive action) against the Board, then attorney fees would be at your expense. If you prevailed and won damages, the lawyer would be paid out of the settlement. I do not see any further avenues available to you in which the association can assist you.

He copied the lawyer and the local and state association presidents.

After reading and re-reading the documented minutes and putting the picture together, I finally realized how they had lied and committed perjury and calumny. I wanted to press charges against the Principal since she was the one to testify. The point is the Superintendent and attorney were managing the meeting's direction but only Pipa and I were sworn in.

One attorney agreed to read the minutes for a fee of $50. He was kind, but again, missed the point. Another attorney I interviewed in April 1999 told me he had quit teaching years before. The final straw for him was when a girl used an expletive against him and that was it; he left teaching. He saw merit in my concerns but did not take my case which surprised me due to his past experience. I do recommend to those planning to teach as a career, to go to law school first. School law is complicated, interpretation can be subjective, and psychobabble is confusing.

I finally documented my grievance on paper to a police officer in the town of my former district to inquire about filing charges. He read my detailed notes but said it was not for Municipal Court. The police captain, who knew me, told me I should get a lawyer because the Principal could counter sue if my charge did not hold up in court. If nothing else, the police now heard the reasons for my dismissal directly from my mouth. Small towns and police officers do protect their own.

Through it all, I was in contact with the state and national association officials. Although one woman at the headquarters in Washington, DC corresponded with me, legal assistance would only come after exhausting help with the state association. I did receive a written response from the national education's President, written by a lawyer, on the President's behalf.

I contacted the Legal Aid office who said I did not qualify for legal aid consultation because I had access to the association. To add insult to injury, the Legal Aid office said they would have met with me if I had been the parent.

In a phone conversation, while she was chewing her lunch, another attorney, recommended by a friend, asked if I was out for vengeance. I told her vengeance belonged to God, but I was seeking justice and to clear my name. Frustrated by all the run-around, I broke down and started crying. I could not get through to anyone just how dangerous my situation was. It was very frustrating to think that lawyers were oblivious of school violence law. Or were they? They treated me as just a defiant, disgruntled employee who had an argument with the Principal.

This sounded contradictory because the first lawyer, in April, advised that ignorance of the law is not a defense. Therefore, if something had taken place on March 24, especially if preventable, I could have been held accountable and "torn apart" on the stand, insubordination charges be damned!

I continued to make regular phone calls to the Trenton offices pleading with them to take a good look at my documentation. They'd probably seen it all before. I was just another victim. But the state President was in contact with me directly and through his secretary, so they were listening. Their motive may have been to protect the jobs of others in the district, but I wanted my name cleared. More than that, I wanted them to realize how flawed it was to shut down a teacher who was addressing the violent behavior of a student. I realized I was not the first one to plow this field.

I reached out to all the names with whom I came in contact. Maybe one person would lobby. Like the persistent woman in the Bible who kept bothering the judge in Luke 18:1-8 till out of exasperation he gave in, I kept going. No gag order existed. Roses can be prickly with those thorns and my middle name is Rose.

The representative for member rights response was this:

> November 24, 1998, Re: The School District:
> I have reviewed your matter and discussed your situation with the association field representative and attorney. I have concluded that there is no likelihood of successful litigation. Therefore, the association will not fund any action.

Although the association kept shutting me down, they must have had a perverse interest in what I had to say: either they were data mining or found me entertaining. I continued to do follow up correspondence and spoke at two association meetings in Trenton, the NJ headquarters.

None of all this was lost on my children. They were in the battle too and showed it in actions and words. That was most encouraging. My daughter wrote me letters each time I spoke to the association. One piece of wisdom from her letter of January 25 before I spoke to the association in person the first time included: "You can do it; you have the power. To give you strength, remember a flower. It pushes hard to find the sun, and then it blooms; it is finally done." Her gem of wisdom: "Bloom where you are planted."

One weeknight on January 26, 1999, my husband drove a former colleague and me to Trenton for a meeting. Both sat in the room but did not say anything. The panel of ten people did not ask them questions. I spoke in detail. I read these words that night from the Association's Teacher Evaluation Handbook of June 1994:

> Evaluation is an issue which intrinsically affects each member. As a positive tool, evaluation can aid teaching staff when they need guidance. Negatively, evaluation can be used to threaten employees and their livelihoods. We cannot be satisfied with

simply coping with the evaluation regulations. We must work actively to ensure that members' rights are protected and that the evaluation process in each district is fair. This is an issue which can make us stronger. We must work together, united.

"United we stand, divided we fall" is a phrase that dates back to the revolutionary time of our nations, popularized in ad campaigns. It holds true if we have empowered those who are power hungry, inept, or just plain evil. Leaders who have a good sense of themselves do not need to divide and conquer. And my former school district administration used what worked to keep the teachers in line. Although I had verbal agreement in March, by April that support was silenced. Why? Because the lie was perpetrated?

In the *Early Warning Timely Response: Guide to Safe Schools,* the experts summarized the message by saying, "Everyone who cares about children, cares about ending the violence." It is time to break the silence that too often characterizes even the most well-meaning school communities. Safety is everyone's job. Teachers, administrators, parents, community members, and students all must commit to meeting the challenge by getting help for children who show signs of being troubled ... We cannot help the children if we cannot help ourselves.

The chain of command directs the teacher to the principal. If there is a rupture in this chain, then the children cannot be protected as they should be ... On December 1, the Press of AC: The parents of the children who were killed in Paducah, Kentucky, said, "They felt forsaken because people do not know what to say or do." The principal of the high school stated the teachers also try to be much more aware of students that do not seem to adjust to high school or kids that are troubled and why they are troubled, that is very much on their minds.

In my case, the principal made me the enemy of the child, his parents and to the Board of Education. Does the association think that I am the enemy? Unfortunately, clearing my name and seeking justice at this point involves a lawyer. Please help me seek justice and help clear the way for other teachers who have the courage to speak out to stop the silence.

I waited for concrete answers, but none came from that meeting. I persisted, appealed and had another opportunity scheduled for April 24. April 20, 1999, would be one year from the incident. With legal time constraints, I only had a year to file charges against the principal. Securing April 24 for a date seemed like a failure but since I had filed for unemployment, I wanted representation.

My husband and young son accompanied me that Saturday. My son paid attention and asked me later, "Why did the fat man laugh when you were talking?"

However, my colleague who had accompanied me in January was becoming distant and did not join me for the meeting on April 24. I had called the local television station before leaving to see if they would cover the appeal, but they did not cover stories that they considered not in the immediate area. I realized I had spoken to a naïve news director. That television station is no longer in existence.

Larger than the room for the January meeting, the room was filled. I was not sure if it was to have been a confidential meeting, but one thing was for sure: with over one hundred people, it was not private and was once again held in Trenton. We overheard a conversation between the state Association President and someone else, that the District Attorney had made a mistake when I had called their office. What mistake?

The breaking news was not lost on any of us in that room. I did not write a speech, but I read a letter given to me by my daughter. She asked them to take a stand with me. They listened and asked questions for over an hour—much longer than the fifteen minutes I expected it to be. I shared my story and showed headlines. I was appealing the decision to shut me down to the attorney and the decision of January 1999 to use the same representative. I had applied for the unemployment insurance in March 1999, so I wanted an attorney to accompany me to the DOL because I thought I would need a lawyer with me.

On April 29, 1999, I received their decision.

As you know, the association executive committee heard your appeal on the issues concerning the Board of Education. The committee considered the facts in the matter as well as the merits of any legal action.

After discussion, it was decided to uphold the decision of the Professional Rights and Responsibilities committee. Therefore, the association shall not provide funds for any further legal assistance. However, Mr. McC shall continue efforts to have pertinent materials removed from your files.

We share your concern for the safety of educators and other school employees and are grateful for you bringing this matter to our attention.

Sincerely yours, Michael

They agreed to help clear my name but would not give me an attorney? They assigned a new representative. He did try a little: I was notified by certified letter that my record was not expunged but my file was "retired." No one could explain that term.

I did succeed in one area though. The two union representatives whom I first contacted had retired from their positions. The association President did not take any legal action that I knew of with the Prosecutor's office; neither did he suggest a rally, protests, or job actions. But he did write this after Columbine. After April 20, did he understand that "yesterday's news" will be "tomorrow's headlines"?

The Columbine Message - our shared obligation:

Regardless of how much time passes, the Columbine High School tragedy will remain in our hearts and our minds. We may never learn the answers to the scores of questions raised by this terrible event. And certainly, the families and friends of the children and teacher who lost their lives will forever ask themselves why this happened. To all those in the Columbine family, we express our sympathy and sorrow. Since April 20, a number of schools in New Jersey have had to deal with bomb scares, threats of violence, menacing e-mail messages, and students mimicking the actions of the students who performed this horrible act. The school community has an obligation to put the safety of its students and staff first whenever a threat is made. The association believes that swift and clear action is the responsibility of the Board of Education, the local administration, and the school staff. We believe it is imperative that all threats are reported to the local police. To withhold this information is folly and could result in a terrible tragedy. If a threat to the students or staff safety is called into a school, the first course of action should be the evacuation of the building. All staff and children should be directed to leave the premises immediately. Search of the building should be done under the direction of the local police. School staff should not be asked to remain in the building or to participate in the search. They're not trained to take on this responsibility. They are, however, the best people to keep the children safe, calm, and out of harm's way once they have left the building. We recognize that every district is required to provide 180 days of schooling each year and that school closings because of threats interfere with the calendar. A school calendar should never take precedence over the safety of our children and staff. School boards and school staff must be ready and willing to establish alternate school days if necessary. We all have an obligation to teach children right from wrong. Teachers already incorporate these values into the curriculum through the study of literature, history, philosophy, and ethics. But that is clearly not enough. Parents and other adult role models must play their part. President Clinton has called for a national discussion of our culture and the messages the media and others send to our children. As citizens we have a responsibility to join in that discussion.

The tragedy at Columbine High School demands a renewed commitment from all of us to all of our children. As national association President Robert Chase said last week, "None of us can be bystanders." America's children count on us to keep them safe, teach them, and help them grow.

On the national association website, it states: "Our students reach their fullest potential when they—and their educators—are healthy and safe in their schools."

Many first consults are free, so I contacted several, even years after. Lawyers, taught to argue both sides, depend on that philosophy for their bread and butter. I buttered bread a few times but never had a lawyer take my case seriously. They do, however, chase the ambulance after a massacre.

Myth: All lawyers understand their oath to the Constitution.

RED HEARINGS

When I received the sworn testimony, I wrote comments on the page borders as I was reviewing the minutes. It took months, though, before the vegetable juice cocktail kicked in. Pipa had introduced material which did not apply to the work with the boy. In her chronology, she had redirections from the fall which were, as everyone noted, not in my file. That meant, on technical grounds alone, the hearing could have been stopped at the beginning, but then they would not have been able to finish their game, and I would not have had this journey. Neither the Board Secretary nor my Association representative stopped the meeting.

Excerpts from the beginning of the hearing:

Association Rep to the Board Attorney: Would you tell us what documents the Board has?
Board Attorney: We have four. We have a packet that we're giving to you.
Association Rep: These are things that we haven't seen. We reviewed the personnel file this morning, and they're not in there.
Pipa: She's in possession of all that but it's not in the file. It is not in the file.
Association Rep: Just right up front, okay, Marian did review her personnel file this afternoon. The only thing in her personnel file were letters of determination and evaluations. None of

this, as we speak, as of this morning, was part of her personnel file.

Board Secretary: The only other thing that we have that we'll be referring to would be what I will call a chronology that Pipa has prepared for tonight's meeting. It just goes through the three incidents that we're talking about and puts them in chronological order for everybody.

Pipa and I disagreed on discipline techniques, teacher responsibilities with after-hours calls to parents and letters sent home. She put her concerns in writing, calling them redirections, but I challenged them. I had already written my first concerns about the troubled boy around this time also, which did not make the school psychologist or Pipa happy.

Upon receipt of the redirections in September 1997, I informed Pipa that, if they were to go into my professional file, I would file a grievance as permitted through contractual agreement. I asked her if the Superintendent had seen them because the Superintendent would have had a hard time with the tone of the letters. At that point in the fall, I did not suspect that they were retaliating. It was too soon for me to see just how far the administration would go in breaking that law. Pipa told the Board I cried and pleaded not to have the September letters put in my file, and so she didn't. At the same time, signatures would have been necessary, which were not on them when shown to the Board. The fact that they did not go in my file speaks to their actual lack of validity.

I gave the association officer copies of the letters that I received throughout the year, which were not signed and not in my file. When he had his own conversation with the Superintendent, I believe he discussed them. I gave them to him to show the pattern of retaliation, which by April 1998 I discerned was the motive of the administration. Did he inform the administrators that I showed them to him? Why else would the principal present them in her chronology to the BOE? Had he introduced red herrings into the situation and then the information was used intentionally to mislead or distract the Board? By now, reflecting on the pattern that I read in the minutes, I realized I should have reported the early redirections and side chats in the Principal's office to the association's county office in the fall. Would the association representative's response have been different then? New Jersey State law protects teachers from unsigned forms, reprimands, or anything added to a file without acknowledgment. I should have refused to participate but I answered all concerns in good faith that the Board's intentions were honorable.

However, it was becoming abundantly clear to me as I reread the minutes that the discussion was solely meant to paint a picture of me as a troublemaker and an uncaring teacher. No one cared about the disturbances the child was causing that could lead to harm or litigation. I was the "problem child." As was the case, no one mentioned all the rewards systems I utilized for positive reinforcement.

The redirections were distractions and used to manipulate the listeners on the Board. It took soul searching, my own research, and prayer for me to come to terms not only with the outcome, but also with how they reached their decision.

CHAPTER 13

PRIVATE AND PUBLIC INTERSECTIONS

Lawyers want cash settlements for their clients but a stable revenue source I was not. Nevertheless, I wanted my story told to continue to bring awareness to my former school district, parents, association and the community. Resigned to reality, with no desire running through my system to return to the school, I drafted a public resignation letter. As I was writing it, news flashed that an emotionally disturbed man killed two security police officers in the U.S. Capitol.

That heightened my desire to use my voice on the printed page. Drafted in July, my resignation letter made it to the paper on October 8, 1998. Part of my public letter went as follows.

> As a schoolteacher, I have often used Rosa Parks as an example of someone who sat down to stand up for her beliefs. She remains a favorite of mine, because her simple gesture sparked a momentous change in our culture. Parker Palmer in his book *The Courage to Teach*, paraphrased Rosa Park's feelings as "being simply tired, tired in her heart and her soul, tired not only of racism but of her own complicity in the diminishing effects of racism. At the age of forty-two, Rosa Parks decided that she could no longer participate in something that violated her own integrity." Parker explains that people like Rosa Parks, who start movements do not do so because they hate an institution, but because they love it too much to let it descend to the lowest form.

I believe we must turn to the example set by the Rosa Parks of this world with the difficult situations in our lives. Therefore, as someone who for many years has loved public school teaching, I am announcing my decision to leave. After receiving disciplinary action last year for speaking out on my students' behalf and then being removed from my classroom, I realized that the freedom to address serious issues does not exist when one is employed by a school district.

The violence is a sign that our culture is descending to its lowest form where children kill children. Even one incident last year or the ones that have gone unnoticed in the past, should have been enough, but we have become a culture of acceptable violence.

On Wednesday, Oct 7, 1998, the Press of Atlantic City ran an article about the school district adopting a policy on weapons:

Before Monday night, the local School Board had nothing on the books detailing what steps staffers should take when discovering a student has a weapon at school ... "It was highlighted by acts around the country," said Board Member E.T. "We wanted to make sure we had a policy in place in case we ever had a situation like that." ... This is something everyone said, "Hey, we should have had this all along but did not see the need for it until these cases were highlighted."

December 18, 1999, Permission was requested, and I was granted to speak to the BOE once again. The first female to vote against me months earlier now spoke of destructive behaviors at games held in the gymnasium. I summarized to the Board developments in my case to-date, which included obtaining the Board minutes.

I am here to address matters of public concern. On April 20, 1998, as an employee, I went to a closed-door hearing, in good faith, that the reprimand I received dated March 31, 1998, was valid and that the hearing would clear up concerns ... Legally

I did not violate a special education law or any New Jersey statute on discipline. According to our teachers' contract and handbook, I did not fail to follow either district procedures or policy. It was stated there was no need for the special teachers to know of my concerns. On page 24 of the handbook, it states that the classroom teachers are responsible for informing special teachers of any emotional or physical problems extant in their class. On page 17, the responsibility when the nurse is not in the building is explained. Nowhere does it state that one teacher can be singled out for not making phone calls at night. Nor can a teacher be singled out to have all correspondence checked before sending letters home.

I responded to all concerns, but I should not have, and advice to the contrary was lacking. The teachers' contract clearly states that no separate files should be kept on an employee. Also, every evaluation is to be signed by the employee, and the employee is to be given a chance to respond in writing ... I felt my Constitutional rights, as well as those of the children in my class, were violated. I chose to officially resign August 26, 1998. It was not an easy decision. In fact, I suffered a miscarriage that day.

Tonight, I am offering a copy of the testimony of April 20, 1998, back to the public's Board of Education in the care of Mr. T. Maybe you can read it and revisit the issues concerning the philosophy of the schools, contracts, and the integrity of the system which you thought I had violated. Please read a *Guide to Safe Schools*, the discipline information from the National Center of Learning Disabilities and the Statewide Advocacy Network. Please note the following excerpts regarding teachers' rights:

"The right to have an atmosphere conducive to teaching. The right to set firm limits on all students needing them. The right to ask for assistance with specific needs. The right to caring and supportive colleagues. The right to physical safety. The right to be valued by the students, the school, and the community."

In regard to the philosophy of the school district, the Principal stated, "It is a teacher who I am trying to bring to come along with us to fit into the philosophy of our schools and, unfortunately, I do not know if Mrs. Carlino has the ability to be remediated to do that; I do not know." To the School Board attorney, "I am neither a priest nor a rabbi," as he compared me within the minutes, but I am a teacher whose philosophy of life is based on God's Ten Commandments. I have based my entire teaching career on that same foundation.

The attorney told me they could not discuss the matter because of "pending litigation." Was that the litigation that should not cause me to lose sleep? He did not say. I stayed for the whole meeting. One parent had shown up to support me. Mr. Tee was not there, so I handed the copy to Mr. Willis.

My revelations to the School Board must have sent them reeling, I could tell by their faces. They had given me time to present even though I was not an employee or resident. By the beginning of April 1999, the Superintendent and the School Board attorney had submitted their resignations citing personal reasons. The Superintendent was leaving by April 30, and the attorney was leaving at the end of the school year. Several former coworkers and parents confirmed the news which had been published. Jezebel was leaving and getting out of town quickly. The newspaper did not report but former coworkers revealed that the Superintendent had an affair with a primary contractor for the new building, a married woman whose husband was a retired Superintendent in another district.

Like a Venn diagram, our circles intersect. I would see Board members in the grocery store or at church, as well as relatives of friends and best friends—the degree of separation was less than 6. One weekday morning at my church, I literally came face to face with Barracuda. I was in the basement after coffee with friends when he opened the door. I did have my chance to tell him off right there and then; but it was his father's funeral. I never hit a man when he is down. I am not sure if he even knew who I was when we came face to face. I said a prayer. It is true when we pray for our enemies, we cannot hate them.

Mr. Tee—the one Board member, who I could tell, knew exactly what was being pulled off on April 20, 1998—and I met a few random times at our respective churches. He seemed afraid of me. I told him he never had to worry about seeing me because, at the meeting that night, he believed me: I could see it in his eyes. If he felt guilty, there was nothing I could do about that.

CHAPTER 14

PSALM 144:1 TRAINING MY FINGERS FOR BATTLE

I spoke and wrote, conscious that teachers, punished for speaking up, will shut down. Confidentiality agreements are detrimental to the truth. Teachers do not park their Constitutional rights at the door of a school building, although administrators and BOE would prefer they did. For an American institution entrusted with passing on knowledge and for the heritage of our nation, why are teachers the ones to retreat from intimidation? I looked to Scripture not only for strength and confirmation, but for battle examples. I did not think of myself as a David, but school districts and the education associations are goliaths.

One night in September 1998, a teacher called wishing me good luck. He asked me about my plans. I told him I was going to write. He recommended that I take a class at the local community college. I did not take him up on his suggestion because I had no extra money to take any course; besides, it was not my direction. However, I did write the whole year and shared my story.

I have learned that, although we are accountable for delivering the message, we are not answerable for how people receive it. Was I used as an example to show other teachers they'd better be quiet? How do we explain the administrators' visceral reactions? If people chose to ignore warnings, then there are costs. When these costs come, the good/evil debate begins. Some answers are difficult to wrap our heads around because the reasons seem surreal.

When I documented, I penned letters to my local district, state, and national representatives, as well as to the U.S. Attorney General, Janet Reno. Reno's office responded with a timestamp on the returned minutes. A friend at church said I had a forum and to use it. You may be surprised that our representatives cannot legally advise or get into the weeds of our problems. Well, maybe if one is a huge contributor, they could.

Ronald Stephens, then the National School Safety Center Executive Director at Pepperdine University was an affirming voice. He and I corresponded through emails. After every school shooting, he was on national television advising "when, not if" a shooting was to occur.

Through the years, I did write editorials about the association, which in reality is a bargaining and lobbying organization. On August 24, 2001, the press published the article "School Violence Is Not a Laughing Matter." I remember how two years ago, when I addressed my concerns about school violence to a gathering of association experts, I was rebuffed, and even laughed at.

The national association decided to offer a survivor's benefit to the families of those "killed in the line of duty." Their decision came after two teachers, Dave Sanders and Barry Grunow, were killed by angry students. The insurance won't save any lives on its own accord but the awareness that teachers are often in the line of fire of angry people brings awareness.

A report from the Department of Education states:

In the four years from 1994 to 1998, 668,000 teachers were victims of violent crimes, including rape: 80,000 of those crimes were considered serious violent crimes. These are just the bare statistics: no emotional damage is considered. And the long-term effect on the witnesses is yet to be considered.

Children are the steppingstones for the politically motivated, so I wrote about school boards too. Not every volunteer is authentically looking out for their best interests; neither is every paid employee. I hear this sentiment increasingly echoed today about "getting involved."

The Current, April 2001: Get to Know Your Candidates before Visiting the Polls

It is school budget election time soon, but more importantly, it is time to vote for school board members. After this past year, we should have learned that it is imperative to be concerned about the people we elect into office. When we choose people with integrity, who do not hide behind their lawyers, then we can be more certain that the budget requests are honest and fair.

Although many may select to ignore local elections, they do so at risk. The decisions rendered by local officials, volunteer or not, impact the lives of each and every member they represent. In addition to monetary consideration, school boards decide curricula, administration, teachers, staff and programs directly affecting our children. Their determinations have ripple effects beyond their city limits.

Votes are made in public, but many discussions are not, and the voters have little input from others because school board meetings are poorly attended, even by the press. Therefore, it is important to know something about the candidate before you vote. Are your candidates leaders in activities with children? How do they respond to the children on a regular basis? Does your candidate have children in school? Does your candidate know the staff as well as administration? What is the candidate's motivation to be on the school board? Will the candidate investigate all the facts before voting? Will the candidate admit when a mistake has been made? Will the candidate volunteer for a criminal background check as mandated for paid district employees?

We cannot continue to ignore local school board elections or the personalities of those who seek public positions. In addition to operating multimillion dollar budgets, school boards are coping with life and death decisions. Make sure you know who's making the educational choices for your children.

History repeats itself. I often repeated my message too. The motivation for the editorial below was based on an October 30, 2008, article about a teacher hurt by a female student in a city about six miles from where I lived. The editorial of mine was published in both papers in my region.

The Current, November 12, 2008, and The Atlantic City Press, November 7, 2008

A most dangerous aspect of teaching in public education today is exemplified by the statements issued by the administration to staff and students regarding talking to the press after any violent incident. School violence is a matter of public concern. It is a shame that our school system can continue to teach the opposite of freedom of speech in the name of not releasing information. Since many people who run for higher office start their careers as school board members, shouldn't we be concerned—dare I say—afraid of policies restricting public comments?

Myth: Restricting public comments always helps with the narrative.

CHAPTER 15

TRIGGERING LAWS

I reviewed gun control laws for legal change but left that path. There were so many laws already in place. Not only do I appreciate the Second Amendment and its purpose, but even a cursory look at the laws showed that the restrictions are on the law-abiding citizens and not the criminal minds. No, controlling the trigger is personal. We would otherwise have to outlaw knives, body parts, planes, trains and automobiles to prevent violence.

Does micromanaging our lives with more and more rules, regulations, and mandates make us safe? New gun laws are not the answer, but we see gun control advocates using every large-scale incident to take away the rights of others. Many states have very strict laws; yet people die because the weapon was illegally used, illegally owned or obtained through inappropriate access, possession or use of a firearm.

In 2000, the Million Mom March on Mother's Day in Washington attracted hundreds of thousands of people. Like any celebrity driven event, it became "a happening." The mayor of my town was organizing transportation from the area and assumed I wanted to go. I am not a fan of protests in general, although I do realize they have their place in society. However, this protest was organized to push for stricter gun control laws with which I disagreed. Focusing strictly on the weapon of choice misses the point. So, I was spending Mother's Day at home. When we are busy, our children fall through the cracks.

Red flag laws can be beneficial, yet in corrupt hands or courts, law abiding citizens can be railroaded. Red flag laws and even the Danger Will Robinson robot from the *Lost in Space* television series circa the 1960s may not have stopped these tragedies. In most massacres, the perpetrators do announce their plans. How many times did the Parkland shooter have to tell people he was going to kill?

At Columbine, the massacre planners, who were flagged, targeted the entire school population with homemade bombs and guns as weapons of choice. The two students were able to smuggle in propane tanks and an arsenal of weapons right under the adults' noses. One would wonder who was minding the store—or at least the cafeteria. The library and the cafeteria were targeted. Why? Do we outlaw duffle bags or pipes?

An edited version of an essay I wrote made it to the editorial page in 2006. My title: "Controlling the Trigger." The editor selected a different title: "Living in a Gun Culture Carries Responsibilities."

The two guns were pointed at a car as I drove along a tree lined street in a white middle-class community. As though in slow motion, I watched as the triggers were pulled and heard the ammunition pop. No target was hit, this time. The weapons of choice were two fully loaded cap guns held tightly in the tiny hands of two boys about six years old. The children were sitting on their front porch, seemingly prepared to "take down" every car that passed by.

As I drove past, I was reminded of my youth. Even as a young girl, I had a toy gun. Much to my mother's chagrin, my sisters and I received plastic rifles. We were granted permission to play with them, but with strict instructions to never aim the guns at anyone. We did not have cap guns, but we did have the caps. I can still smell the gunpowder and hear the popping sounds as we hit the little red dots on rocks and saw the spark.

I turned my car around at the next street and drove back to the house of the young "snipers." They did not seem alarmed when I approached to knock at the front door. The woman who answered the door pleasantly did not take offense when I talked to her about my concerns. As I left, I saw her motion to them to go into the backyard.

Stopping at the self-service gas station on an Interstate, my husband pumped the gas as the rest of us took a bathroom break. While waiting our turns in the well-stocked convenience mart, I purchased a copy of USA TODAY, whose lead story was about the survivors of the Columbine High School massacre. My son, who was then nine, and his hockey teammate took a fancy to a small display of water pistols. As they aimed and shot at each other, they discovered, much to their delight, that the toys were loaded. After using each other for a brief target practice, the water guns were turned on me. "Do not point at anyone and put them down" were my mother's words which I could hear coming out of my mouth.

A brother of a gunshot victim founded the organization, PAXUSA, which encouraged parents to check with other parents to see if guns are in a playmate's home, and if they are secured and away from the children. After she read the editorial I wrote about the organization, a close friend told me that a child did pull a gun on her daughter when she was babysitting years before. No one was hurt. ASK is not a judgment of gun owners. People have the right to own guns and use them recreationally and in self-defense. Don't Be Afraid to ASK for Answers.

Do we wait for mayhem? I was trying to make sense of the violence and find evidence of failed protection. I pulled out a book because of its title. I had never heard of this school shooting by an adult in 1988, a full ten years earlier. The school's name was similar to my junior high, Hubbard. The last name of the detective in the story was the same as a Board member's name—Detective Tee. The Illinois city's name was a third connection.

The Current, August 8, 1999: Violence More Than a Law Enforcement Problem

On May 20, 1988, in an elementary school, a lone female walked into the building, hid ammunition and weapons, then at point blank range killed one child and seriously injured five others. When she left, she entered a nearby home, taking a family hostage and shooting another victim. The thirty-year-old white woman died of a self-inflicted gunshot wound.

I found the book selection after this past July 4 weekend (1998) when the news told of barbecues, fireworks and gunfire. In several Chicago suburbs and Bloomington, IN, the holiday ended with reports of three people dead and eight injured, all at the hands of one person. The sniper, who committed suicide by gunshot, was a twenty-year-old white male.

The woman, diagnosed with obsessive compulsive disorder (not necessarily associated with violence) at a young age, attended special education classes as a student. She was described as exhibiting ritualistic behaviors which became bizarre as an adult. She stabbed her ex-husband with an ice pick a year or so before the killings. However, the authorities did not believe him because the woman and her father convinced the detective otherwise.

On the morning of May 20, 1988, she delivered and sent arsenic laced treats and drinks to various homes and set a friend's home on fire with the intent to kill. According to the biography, the arsenic, which she had stolen, had a weak solution, while the mother and children in the house which she set on fire were able to escape.

For the most recent Chicago shooter, a red flag, the paper said, had been placed in his file at his university. A former girlfriend documented domestic violence reports. He belonged to a noted racist group and distributed hate propaganda.

Although many knew the female's rituals and strangeness, few indicated, when interviewed, that they would have predicted the violence. Some stated the same about the male. Before the murders, the woman's ex-husband and the man's ex-girlfriend knew differently.

The authors concluded that gun control would be the woman's legacy. According to them, in 1989 the Illinois General Assembly amended the state's firearm laws to prohibit "violent, suicidal, threatening or assaultive" individuals from obtaining or holding firearm owners identification cards—FOIA. The 1988 killer had been able to purchase the guns legally with the parents' credit cards even though the police were aware of some of her violent episodes.

In 1999, the male assaulter did not have the legal right to buy guns. Denied a gun at a licensed gun shop, he obtained weapons of choice at an unlicensed dealer. Both of their suicides left unanswered questions. The gun laws of Illinois may have prevented the unlawful purchases of guns this past Independence Day weekend, but that law was circumvented, as has been shown to be the case in many of the schoolyard massacres.

The authors of *Murder of Innocence: The Tragic Life and Final Rampage of Laurie Dann* said that the reporters who covered the story, blamed the shooter's parents, the police department and the doctors who treated her. The town commemorated the shooting's thirty-year anniversary in 2018. A student reflected, in an essay, about being a survivor, thirty years after the murder.

The author, Rick Ayers, in *An Empty Seat in Class: Teaching and Learning after the Death of a Student 2015*, has a chapter titled "Our Worst Nightmare." The author highlights excerpts from an interview with, as he states, "my friend, Dick Streedain." In this interview, the Principal describes vividly and in detail when the woman entered his school. When life breaks abruptly, we do remember, if not so traumatized, that our brains shut down all memory. When people try to reconcile the nightmare of reality, death and reactions to it, they often romanticize it.

The Principal's words were these:

... time when we were a healthy school community. We weren't fragmented. We have created a high degree of coherence in the curriculum. We started with class meetings ... I said, find out who's been shot and call their parents. And make sure both parents get called and let them know that something bad has happened. Everybody was very autonomous. They all played to their strengths. When the secretary was told the shooting started, she just started shaking. What do I do? and she thought. I'm just going to start ringing bells. The kids tell the story that when Laurie Dann started shooting she would go boom, boom, boom, then bells ring and she left. You can't really plan for a tragedy like this. Who would say, ring the bells? Every time a kid came back, after the shooting, they had to replay the whole story.

I remember walking down the hallway and thinking I'm the worst Principal in the United States. Six kids got shot, I'm responsible for them, and I'm a phony. There's no way I have the right stuff in me. I'm like a chicken with his head cut off. Suddenly, for some reason a biblical admonition came to me, "The truth will set you free." Within the period of a minute, I crossed over a line from the most crazy that I'd ever felt to the most calm I'd ever felt. It became very clear. I knew what I needed to do …

Everybody just seemed to know what to do. It just happened. A lot of social workers came over; ministers came over … Some of the rooms had 17 kids and 14 adults. The next morning there were 900 people in the auditorium. I was not sad or nervous about it, though in a normal situation I would be … One of the most important ingredients for our ability to move through our school tragedy was a school culture that placed a high priority on teacher autonomy.

On the day of the shooting this played out in numerous ways. Teachers felt confident in their ability to make decisions based upon the needs of their children … processing of the event was a natural extension of what was already in place to help children make sense of the daily challenges, hopes, and fears of their everyday experiences.

On the day of the shooting, teachers were able to provide their students with experiences and activities that would help children process the tragedy through classroom meetings, conversations, drawings, block play, and drama. These activities would flow from the questions, concerns, and fears of the individual students as well as the collective community. Teachers felt empowered to draw other available resources (volunteer parents, teacher assistants, student teachers and auxiliary staff) into their classrooms to help work through the many immediate challenges as well as those during the remaining days of the school year.

The description sounds like fantasy. How did later shootings get handled? Failure to report problems can lead to the extreme acts. In January 2024, an actor said in an interview that he was in fourth grade at Hubbard Elementary School in 1988. He reported that his mother had a "gut reaction" not to send him to school that very day. Again, why do we have premonitions? Was there talk in the town of the woman's bizarre behavior before that deadly day?

Autopsies reveal history. The gun is the tool used, not the cause.

Teachers do not like to report as could be seen in the silence at my school. A misplaced idea of sympathy takes over common-sense approaches to discipline. Interestingly, there have been inci-dences of pranks such as one when students added white board cleaning fluid to a teacher's drink. The school officials per the reports called it an "ill-conceived prank." On one such occasion, the teacher did not want to file a police report since "The students meant no harm." However, national news picked up the "prank."

In the Toms River area of New Jersey, a young man hijacked a car. The victim, a female teacher, recorded the conversation in which she pleaded for her life. She said she would not report him; however, she recorded the conversation. Why would the hostage record? She died at his hands, and he was jailed. Her coworkers, when interviewed about their loss, said the dead teacher would not have reported the incident. Do you think there is a problem in this type of thinking?

The greatest mistake we make when it comes to gun posses-sion is assuming that the gun will not be used. But what other laws, besides using a gun to kill, did the perpetrators break?

Myth: Gun control laws will keep people from killing each other.

THORN IN THEIR SIDE

Did they think that I would go quietly and not speak out? If so, they were mistaken. I became a voice in the debate, following the rainbow trail. I lobbied my representatives for changes in a limited number of laws and became a "gadfly" at board and city council meetings. I wrote primarily about prevention, but the topics also included the Open Public Records Act, parenting, the death penalty and divorce. I expressed my knowledge and understanding of the topics. I did not let the sarcasm about everyone having an opinion get me down as I continued to reach out of my comfort zone.

I have a philosophy as in the pop song, "I get knocked down, but I get up again. You are never going to keep me down" (Chumbawamba, Tubthumping, 1997). Righteous anger is a motivator. Trust in God and taking leaps of faith strengthens us. "The way out of a dark mist is over a rainbow trail"—God's rainbow. Of course, many people would have preferred that I just went somewhere else with the message or disappeared completely.

My story is about taking steps before lockdowns. Only the naïve would think we could stop everything evil; but can't we at least try? At first suspicious of me, the local weekly paper and even the regional papers began publishing more of my submissions after the "unthinkable" happened. One editor told me, "Mrs. Carlino, we cannot publish all editorials you submit." If my editorials did not get in, at least one person read the material from 1998 until 2012. I kept being the thorn in the media's side too it appears. In 2012, I started a blog: *From the Teachers Desk* on BlogSpot.

"Sticks and stones may break my bones, but words will never hurt me," an oft-repeated adage from childhood applies to any situation when speaking up. Expect name calling. Besides the incompetent remarks and beyond remediation labels, I was the recipient of more. Standing up for important issues can create enemies among friends, and friends among enemies. I experienced both. For example, I stood next to a father at a hockey game like the elephant in the room, concerns or opinions still not voiced to me at that point. I just looked at him and told him I loved the kids. People kept their distance from me or wouldn't say anything to me. Sometimes I had to break the ice. Other times I just let people think what they wanted of me.

Some people applied the nickname, "Debbie Downer," which was a favorite, after a character who was a buzz killer on Saturday Night Live. A friend told me I was called Father Marian and the Pope, or persona non grata at times. Clearly no one wanted me at their parties. However, I was good at driving their kids and dropping them off at midnight. People trusted me with their children, homes, and dogs, but preferred to pass off my education and insights on breaking news. Maybe I saw too much? The jury is still out.

One person told me if I talked about God, people would think I was crazy. How many prayer services are held after school massacres? An editor referred to me as "Yesterday's News." (He did change his mind, though.)

"Quirky," was the nickname I was twice blessed with by two experts in people skills. The "lack of originality" came from an administrator, Pipa, in our discussion in February 1998 about the "rash" decision to close the old school. She told me to write an editorial about it.

The other name caller was a church leader. He questioned my request for him to meet about an eighth-grade boy in Confirmation class; but he did do as I asked and talked to the parents. A volunteer teacher not trained in education, explained her frustration in trying to maintain discipline by physically separating the group.

I could hear the stress in her voice and see it in her face. For the next rotation, he would be in my group. We joined forces and asked for a meeting. In a religious education program, we had different options. Exile is one form of resolution, but it is hardly the best method. We met and brainstormed with other staff volunteers, regardless of one paid employee who questioned whether we had legal liability. The child causing the stress was an eighth grader, who, when he was in fourth grade, suggested that a swat team could be called to prevent violence. It does help when you are familiar with the children from past experiences and interactions with the family. Intact, faithful families are not free from stress, and sometimes it is reflected directly in the children's behavior or at least in their faces.

Interesting timing that was. The meeting was held in December 2012 with the parents. I was told that the massacre at Sandy Hook was not a motivating factor for the priest to meet with the family, although my coworker and I had asked for the meeting before Sandy Hook became a national controversy.

As another mother and I sat in front of a convenience store, collecting for a sports team, we discussed problems in the schools and our families. I told her that I was not immune from discord, and being a voice in the debate did not offer me protection. Life finds us: we do not have to search it out. I certainly did not remain immune to tribulation in the personal side of my life. The spillover from my work is documented in other court records. "You are an embarrassment" was once said of me, though I'm sure the reasons were not due to my embarrassing behavior.

"Marian R" was another nickname—evidently high school students read my editorials. I was actually impressed with that name to which I am referred even today. As for me, I called myself a thorn.

The kitchen door at the one elementary school in my town was left open so many times, it was hard to count. I complained repeatedly as a parent and as a taxpayer and advocate when my kids graduated. I did vote "no" on a budget one year and told the Board the unattended, open door was the reason. A person of ill intent can always find the weak link in security. Even after our elementary school implemented controlled access, people were still finding ways around the rules.

Regular volunteers had identification but still had to be buzzed in. On the other hand, the PTA (Parent Teacher's Association) President, the wife of a Board member, and her son were walking to a side door. I was holding a baby. As she approached the door, which was unlabeled, I told her she should use the main door. Her son, who was no longer a student there, agreed with me. She turned around, pointed her hand at me, gun style, and said, "Yeah, and I have a gun too." Evidently, she knew the door was accessible, unlocked, and at the back end of school near the gymnasium hallway. Her response did make me wonder all the more since we worked very well together. What note did I hit to receive such a reaction? Every child at some point in time uses their fingers to shoot at something—but an adult?

So, I documented this incident in writing to the Superintendent, well aware that the parents' group president's husband sat on the School Board and was an usher at my church. Those who volunteer should not be exempt from following safety procedures that do not take any rights away.

It was this theme that motivated a teacher, tired of lockdowns and active shooter drills scaring children, to author *The Elephant in the Room, a Lockdown Story.*[13] It's a story using animals escaping from a circus train as the uninvited visitors. I believe the title has a double meaning. My question when I read this was why was the door unlocked for the animals to gain access?

On May 24, 2022, a gunman entered Robb Elementary School in Uvalde, Texas, through an unlocked door. The doors then became a matter for the investigations. Nineteen children and two teachers were killed. As in every school shooting, controversy swirls. Violence does not make life easy on anyone. Confusion, pain, heartache, the blame game and lawsuits are all common conditions and actions after a large-scale attack, no matter the location. Death shakes our very souls when children are the victims. Schools and the womb, after all, we are told, are the safest places for children—that is, until someone is intent on killing.

As in the police response at Columbine and in Parkland, Florida, investigations of the response by the police has led to criticisms and more investigations. Uvalde made headlines again in January 2024 because of the Department of Justice reports.

Become a thorn and ask questions. Thorns are an important part of the rose's story.

CHAPTER 17

WHEN LIFE
HANDS YOU LEMONS

People asked me if I was collecting unemployment. I was bewildered. I had never collected compensation because teachers do not collect unless fired or laid off. I left my job and was not fired. Brick walls seemed to constantly be in my path. Not one attorney, nor the consultants, suggested I go the unemployment route.

Then, one day my husband came home from work with words of wisdom. A coworker of his had mentioned that she had received unemployment compensation because she "left her job with good cause attributable to the work." That woman left due to pregnancy. I saw an open door and some hope.

In March 1999 I applied for the benefits. I had not missed that deadline! The DOL representative cautioned me that I would be denied at first because I resigned, but that I should keep appealing the decision. After I explained my situation, she actually asked me, "What took you so long to get here?" as she photocopied the 126 pages of minutes. Sure, enough, my claim was rejected. The appeal process involved more sworn tape testimony which, I realized, was good because a representative from the school district would have to testify.

The district did not send anyone to the first appeal, so my hour long sworn testimony was uncontested. I did not have any witnesses, but I gave a long list of all the teachers, the administration and parents to the claims examiner. He told me that it was the quality of my testimony that counted, not the quantity.

I received notice that I was indeed entitled to compensation and checks retroactive to the original claim date. The checks came in just at the right time because my husband had left his job. That day in late May 1999 I lay down on the sofa in a fetal-like position to pray.

Within ten days of my receiving the first checks, the School District attorney sent an appeal to the unemployment board challenging my compensation on the grounds they had never received written notification. Once deceitfulness sets in, the truth is not a priority. My checks kept coming as I prepared for another appeal. By this time, I was certain I would succeed at the next round because, to contest my testimony, the district would have to lie with my witnesses present. If I lost an appeal at this level, the next step would be a Superior Court. I was prepared to go there alone. At the second Appeal Tribunal, the district sent the business administrator who had been hired after I left. She would not testify against me. The district had argued in their appeal that I was not entitled to unemployment since I had resigned and sent a copy of my resignation of August 26. They could have just as well sent the copy of my public resignation because my resignation was no secret.

My first testimony stood. Asked if I wanted to add anything, I did not. In July 1999, the New Jersey State Department of Labor awarded the final appeal. All was now documented in another court of law: I was entitled to compensation.

> While an employer is entitled to set standards of performance, he is also obligated to use common courtesy in dealing with his workers. When he delivers a harsh reprimand in the presence of others, he violates that obligation. A worker is entitled not only to his wages but also to the preservation of his dignity. When he fails to receive either, he has good cause attributable to such work for quitting.
>
> The decision of the Appeal Tribunal must be based on competent evidence. The employer was provided an opportunity to offer competent evidence, but their witness had no firsthand knowledge of the incidents. Therefore, the Appeal Tribunal is

bound by the available competent evidence, the sworn tape testimony of the claimant. The claimant's testimony that the reprimand was unwarranted remains unrefuted. She was removed from her classroom while her students were present and had good cause attributable to the work for leaving. Therefore, no disqualification applies under N. J. S. A. 43: 21-5 (a)_, as claimant did not leave the job voluntarily without good cause attributable to such good work. The matter of the claimant's eligibility for benefits during reported weeks of unemployment is remanded to the Deputy for an initial determination.

Decision: No disqualification applies under N. J. S. A. 43: 21-5(a)_ as the claimant did not leave the job voluntarily without good cause attributable to such work. The determination of the Deputy is reversed 7/19/1999.

Do you believe in coincidences or does God wink? Sitting in a pew, well after the final DOL decision, was the woman who first took my claim. Her nephew's family were active parishioners and employed in my church. I thanked her and, although I do not remember her name, I do remember her words and face.

As I reread the Appeal Tribunal decision, I read one phrase time and again: my testimony was "competent." It implied they had used harsh punishment on me. The sworn testimony at the Department of Labor countered the label of incompetence.

Life changes, no matter how they come about, can be sour. After all the appeals, I enrolled in classes through the DOL to learn how to run a small business. I hoped to establish a small publication regarding educational trends. The accounting class taught me that running a business takes time, talent, and treasure! Finding the treasure was harder than I thought it would be.

"When Life Hands You Lemons" is the short essay I read to my fellow classmates in the training program offered through unemployment in 1999.

They say when a life experience is a downer, you have been handed a lemon. Unemployment, without a doubt, can be one of those sour times. Losing or leaving a job is a life altering condition because your current course of thinking has been changed.

The lemon analogy involves a recipe for success: make lemonade. If you use only the lemon, you still end up with a sour taste. Add other ingredients to make your lemonade tasty.

The main ingredients are friendly support (the water) and unemployment compensation (the sugar). Incorporate enhancers like the training programs offered through the state Department of Labor.

Instructors share expertise, and classmates, holding similar lemons but different recipe ideas, bring advocacy. Free hours of professional consultations and access to computer classes add a twist. The new information guides the unemployed worker to become an entrepreneur! You may not be ready to sell your recipe at a stand, but the lemonade is sweet.

In 2012, before Hurricane Sandy hit NJ, I facilitated a class, retraining the long term unemployed on how to search for employment opportunities. I truly enjoyed the experience. I worked with adults, who were mandated to take one class. I instructed the class, while a representative of the NJ Department of Labor supervised attendance. She informed me that the interviewers/examiners at the appeals level are lawyers. That piece was affirming. All along I had prayed for faithful, prayerful and/or affordable lawyers! The DOL was free; one out of three is not bad!

CHAPTER 18

WATERSHED EVENTS

In Thurston High School, Springfield, Oregon, May 21, 1998, Kip Kinkel, wearing a tan trench coat, opened fire in his school's cafeteria. His parents, both teachers, had bought the guns for him. They died when their son pulled the trigger before he went to school. His sister lived through the nightmare. Think of it with 20/20 hindsight: parents bought guns trying to appease a mentally ill teenager?

That night I made a phone call to a family member, my brother-in-law, who taught in a high school in northern NJ. I told him I knew the reason the shootings happened because teachers like me were getting shut down while others kept quiet.

In 2018, a documentary aired on KLLC calling it "one of the earliest modern day" school shootings. The reporter did not do his research.

On the weekend before April 20, 1999, our community hosted a hockey tournament. The kids and adults were out of hand. The kids sitting in the bleachers were yelling names at our own coaches. I turned around to an adult from our city who was encouraging the insults. The man told me, "Mrs. Carlino, they are not in church." I prayed a lot that weekend. The event was full of behavioral problems to the extent that my husband who had refereed the cadet level tournaments came home that Saturday night and said our son would never play cadet level street hockey. He eventually had to live up to those words.

I had fallen asleep on the sofa the day the news broke from Colorado. My children were already home due to the time difference with us living on the east coast. My daughter woke me with the words, "Mommy, Mommy, it's happening again!"

The doorbell rang shortly thereafter. It was a coach asking to speak with me about a situation in the town's sports team leadership. I agreed that the issue had to be addressed. He was a member of our community council and a coach for hockey. I do think he saw the relevancy of knocking on my door the same day as Columbine was breaking news. Had he prayed the weekend before too?

On April 20, 1999, I sat and listened to the voices in shock because two students executed their plans to kill. Twelve students and one teacher died as the shooters opened fire in the cafeteria, hallways, and library. Twenty-three other students were wounded, many critically. The massacre had been planned for a year. The rampage lasted one hour before the killers committed suicide.

The shooting at Columbine High School was personal. Although it was not the first shooting after I left teaching, it was the most violent up to that point within those few years and one year to the day that I was called "incompetent."

The Principal of that school, who was interviewed on national television that fateful night, stated for all to hear that there was no history of problems with the students who planned and conducted the massacre. I wanted to scream, whether he was in shock, denial, or covering up, years of study proved his statement wrong. I called him a liar from the start. Bullying was blamed for the extreme vengeance, but that has been disputed. The shooters had been "losing" it for quite a while. The heartache was just the start of it. Even the victims became victims again from stress that developed; some were shunned for asking questions and expecting answers.

The school closed after the shootings and did not reopen until the following year. They had a pep rally televised nationally when they returned. Personally, I thought the rally was in poor taste. The football chants were meant to reunite but broken hearts do not repair with pep rallies. With every massacre since, there is always a comparison. The "Columbine Effect" became the benchmark.

"Copycat crime" was often used in describing later shootings. Instead of a term used in child's play, it became one to explain deaths in schools.

The files were sealed after the massacre. The response times of law enforcement was criticized because the police waited to go into the building. The question of missed warning signs of juvenile records was raised. Beside carnage, a paper trail of both students was left behind. According to the a probation officer of Eric Harris, one of the attackers had ideas of suicide and homicide. The false teaching of confidentiality that hinders sharing information facilitated the planning and follow- through that led to the murders, suicides, and injuries. Only those charged with supplying weapons served any time.

On April 20, 1999, I called the former Board attorney's office and told the secretary to tell Barracuda that the shooting was a type of utter failure that I had wanted to prevent the year before. When all celebrities, legal experts and talking heads, including Vice President Gore, met in Littleton, I called the national education association's executive office. To my surprise, they answered the phone. I asked if the national association's President was to visit Columbine, the President of the association attended.

We have come a long way in security measures. However, guards, metal detectors, name badges, and stricter rules have not stopped some pretty noteworthy shootings. Lockdown, drills, evacuation and codes are everyday terms from preschool through college. And yet, after every offense, no matter how extensive the security measures are, the detailed scrutiny always points to a missed sign.

The telling thing is people will state outright that when a suspect is identified, it is not a shock. Jesus said we can read the signs of weather with storms brewing but we cannot see the signs involving people. Of course, not every event can be prevented; some can only have the effects minimized. But with the rigor with which Columbine was studied, with guest appearances, books, interviews, tributes and new organizations, one would think that the learning may have prevented other massacres. At a band concert, a seemingly wise and reasonable band director allowed two eighth grade students to dress up in black trench coats as part of a skit. I walked out in protest. One of those students had a reputation of being a player and extorting others to give him answers for tests—only an eighth grader, mind. Timing is everything. Years pass before authorities release reports. Disclosure lags. Columbine was like that. So were the issues of the leadership in sports teams in my community before background checks became law in N.J.

In 1999, I reached out to the Violence Institute of New Jersey at UMDNJ because they advertised a Summit on School Violence. I trained with them in order to help facilitate with small groups of teenagers. The students talked and the adults listened and directed the brainstorming meetings on how to stop the violence.

Once a year, the Foundation for Education sponsored a play performed by the fourth through sixth graders. That year *Guys and Dolls*, a Broadway production originally from the 1930s was chosen; I questioned the choice. The play director said he had a problem when *Annie*, a 1977 Broadway production based on the comic strip *Little Orphan Annie*, was selected a few years before. I understood. He used silly string for the closing scene. We worked well together as volunteers.

How many crosses were placed for the dead at Columbine?

Another editorial, "Columbine Lawsuits Highlight District and Parent Responsibility in Preventing School Violence," was published on June 27, 2001.

According to a June 14, 2001, news report, another severely injured student, paralyzed, at Columbine High School filed a lawsuit claiming that the authorities failed to investigate warning signs and threats of physical harm that were occurring at least a year before. The lawsuits coming out are many and not without merit ... Unfortunately, without legal pressure, those who should do not come forward ... It is a different story now because the extreme level of violence has sent shockwaves through us all. I believe that the school district should be held at least partially responsible … School districts are not the only ones on the receiving end of litigation. Parents of children who are causing problems are being sued. Therefore, it is to their benefit to be open to finding solutions to the problems and not turning a "blind eye." Experts in the field studying school violence agreed that the code of silence must be broken to break the cycle … The high school has become a household word and lawsuits abound against those involved.

Without any adults noticing, how did the shooters get bombs in? Pecking orders exist. Tenured verses non tenured, secretaries, aids, janitors, cafeteria workers—who do you think would be on the bottom rung? My guess is the cafeteria staff. Yet, through the course of a day, most see every student. Cafeterias tend to bring out the best in students, right? Low men on the ladder do not report to the President and sometimes it is easier to think with heads in the sand.

This is an excerpt from *Columbine a True Crime Story* by Jeff Krass[14]

If there is a silver lining, at least one solution still stands out: catching the warning signs. And there is almost always some type of sign. Unearthing signs in the days, weeks, months or years before an actual shooting is no easy task. If it were, we would have been able to act many times over. But examining the spectrum of public shootings is our best chance. And as the afterward recounts, it is exactly what four junior high school girls did after Columbine.

The shootings in 1996-97 influenced me. The ones in 1998 reinforced my determination to speak up.

February 2, 1996, Moses Lake, Washington: A fourteen-year-old opened fire in his algebra class killing two students and one teacher; another student was injured.

March 12, 1996, Dunbane, Scotland: When an intruder entered the Dunbane Primary School, sixteen children and one teacher were killed and ten injured. The killer committed suicide.

February 19, 1997, Bethel, Alaska: A student killed a principal and one student and wounded two.

March 19, 1997, Sanas, Yemen: six students and two others were killed at two schools.

October 1, 1997, Pearl Mississippi: A student killed his mother and two students, wounding seven.

December 1, 1997, West Paducah, Kentucky: three students were killed and five wounded as they were praying in a circle at their high school.

December 15, 1997, Stamps, Arkansas: two students were wounded by another student who hid in the woods.

March 24, 1998, Jonesboro, Arkansas: Two boys pulled a fire alarm and lured their schoolmates out to the playground, killing four students and one teacher, and injuring ten.

April 24, 1998, Edinburgh PA: A student opened fire at a school dance, shooting and killing one teacher at point blank range; two students were wounded.

May 19, 1998. Fayetteville, Tennessee: one student killed another student, angry that the victim was dating the shooter's ex-girlfriend.

June 15, 1998, Richmond VA: one teacher and a guidance counselor were wounded by a fourteen-year-old student in a hallway.

The shootings impacted education, the face of which has forever changed. In 1999, the face of the injured student hanging out of Columbine High School's window put a real face to the subject.

How many principals still express the same opinion as the Principal did at the high school in Fayetteville, Tennessee, on May 19, 1998. From ABC News, "You'd never believe it would happen, but it did. It's very sad."

Myth: It cannot happen here.

CHAPTER 19

SIX DEGREES
OF SEPARATION

When I see bright blue skies with no clouds, I sometimes remember that day in September 2001. Who were the real sharks on that day? It was no coincidence that I found the little sign about Noah, "It was not raining when Noah built the ark," which I found while sorting through donated posters at our church office and turned around to show it to the people in the room with me.

The bombings or plane crashes at the World Trade Center, The Pentagon, and Shanksville, PA, were another violent blow to our nation. Just as school districts are still feeling the effects of shootings, our nation has never been the same since September 11, 2001. The

Monday morning quarterbacking showed missed warning signs and other sinister plots. Unfortunately, when warning signs are missed, voices turn to tightening security to the point where our individual rights get compromised and stomped on. Security measures and rules meant to make us feel safer, have managed to restrict our freedoms.

I found a poster with a picture of a runner coming out of a dark cloud. I too was in a figurative dark time. The poster's message, "The way out of a dark mist is over a rainbow trail." What makes people get excited and feel hopeful about a collection of sun-reflected colors in water droplets after a storm? It's all about covenant. That poster graced our family room wall for many years until it was much needed in another family's home. I gave it to my friend as inspiration, never forgetting the message.

On September 10, 2001, a priest had given a homily about our guardian angels and surrendering things in life. I thought he'd got his dates wrong since the Feast Day for our Guardian Angels is October 2 each year. Why would he mention them on September 10? He said surrendering our material goods prepares us for the ultimate surrender of our lives back to God. On September 11, the homily brought brutal reality into frontal view, and erased complacency one more time. I visited an older neighbor and called the school. My nephew had created a family social media webpage. Emotions did not hang back as we reached out to make sure everyone was OK. Not one person was unaffected in one way or another. Another nephew witnessed people jumping; our church secretary's family member worked in one of the buildings; my sister-in-law was a flight attendant. My sister lived in Pittsburgh; my college roommate worked in downtown Washington, D.C., and my neighbors worked for the FAA. I loved NYC and visited often. Fighter jets took off from the air base at the FAA Tech Center, just west of Atlantic City a few miles from my house.

My daughter and son were in school. I called the offices to advise "This is not good." Asking them to pray was a no brainer; they were members of my church. Administration limited television coverage for them while working but everyone prays when in a foxhole no matter the laws.

We may have all been wrong about the "Whodunit" of 9/11 but one thing was for sure: I did not want to see vengeance taken. Vietnam was still etched in my memory.

What are the real puzzle pieces to any life altering world event?

How did 9/11 factor into school safety?

When it was time for my children to go to college, I wanted them to pick a campus location near family or close enough to home, so it would not involve a long trip. We cannot really protect them from the real world: we have to prepare them. However, we can plan on things that are controllable such as having family nearby in case of an emergency. So true because both of their college campuses experienced certain degrees of violence!

I reached out to an administrator at my son's campus after one student was killed on a street. That man lived the nightmare in 2000 at Seton Hall University when a fire, criminally set, killed three students and injured fifty-eight. The word "prank" was used to describe the actions. Has ownership of matches been criminalized?

In 2005, a young man went missing at his college—I knew his grandparents. It took months before they finally found his remains in a landfill. How did he fall down a garbage chute?

In 2006, a friend called me to say she wanted to take her kids out of the schools. The news sparking that conversation was the hostage taking and killing of girls at an Amish elementary school. The perpetrator was a local man, not of the Amish community. The victim's families offered forgiveness. The perpetrator died. Do you think that the man would not have faced criminal justice if he had lived that day? The movie, *Amish Grace, Lifetime 2010* from the book, *Amish Grace How Forgiveness Transcends Tragedy*[15] told the story. The murderer's wife did write that she was grateful for the grace shown to her.

I was on the phone with my college roommate on April 16, 2007, sitting in my living room with MSNBC on for news. We do not talk often but when we do, we can chat for hours. That day was no different. Since the television was on quietly tuned to the cable news, I noticed an alert come across the screen about a shooting at Virginia Tech. My roommate's son was a senior there. The cameras then zoomed in on the control room at the station which was commenting and studying the breaking news. I had learned enough about news coverage of school shootings that this was not national news because of one death. The coverage was intense. First they reported the two earlier deaths, but I could tell there was more not being told. I asked my roommate if she had talked to her son that morning; I told her there was an emergency, and to call her son and then call me back if she could. She contacted her son and called me back quickly. He was OK. I told her to watch the news because it was bad. My friend's son happened to be at home that day, off campus. A neighbor of his had been killed. But the first young man killed in the dorm was a best friend of a young man we knew. Others killed that day were just six degrees of separation. I was working at a college campus at the time of the shooting at Virginia Tech. It was personal.

It was no less personal to the author of *No Right to Remain Silent*, Lucinda Roy, 2009,[16] a professor at Virginia Tech. The massacre may indeed be yesterday's news to present day educators and the general population, but it is one of the worst massacres in history. How does one mentally ill person pull off such an event? We underestimate the intelligence and intent of people all the time. The professor wrote in retrospect about identified missed signs, administrative reactions, follow up investigations, lawsuits won by families, as well as the silence. In her closing pages this is what she said:

> The right to remain silent must be guaranteed because it functions as a servant of justice. It allows people, especially those who are most vulnerable to abuse, to gain access to assistance. It provides a space in which to reflect before we speak; it enables us to obtain legal counsel. But silence is being used too often these days by those in leadership positions who want to ignore critical questions. It is too easy to clam up, or to leave others to speak up on your behalf, and thus avoid personal risk. When silence is used as a substitute for leadership, communities are obliged to take on that risk themselves.
>
> But speaking up is never easy; there is always a price to be paid. Reading about other school shootings and living so long inside the heads of angry young men has been challenging. I want to read happy books that have beginnings, middles, and ends that don't wound you. I want to laugh like I used to with people I love.

What do we learn from the first-person accounts of shootings? Can we gather from the movies that retell it? How would private eye Peter Falk aka Columbo (1971-2003 NBC and ABC television series) investigate a school shooting?

I woke up on the morning of July 20, 2012, to a headline that fourteen people died, and seventy-eight were injured in a shooting at a theater in Aurora Colorado. I turned on the television to hear a live broadcast from the scene. While the news was assuring people that the shooter was in custody alive, unanswered questions remained about the exact number of victims and extent of the injuries. The gunman confessed to the police that he had rigged his apartment to explode, causing intense security and critical workers to be deployed to deactivate the intricate system of bombs.

Does it take an expert to figure out that the shooter was a genius? Journalists started to do their research. He had recently been a student at the University of Colorado. Pundits blamed guns and the movie *The Dark Knight Rises* (2012 Warner Brothers), which was playing that night. There was a gag order in place on the reports because with an impending trial, publicity would damage any case, but it was learned that a psychiatrist at the University of Colorado had earlier contacted a campus police officer in the past. Psychologists, priests and rabbis do not have legal protection when someone tells them that they are planning to commit murder.

I had not heard the early news reports about Sandy Hook in Newtown, Connecticut. I was standing in the middle of my apartment when my phone rang, and my son asked me, "Are you OK, Mom?"

I said, "Yes, what's going on?"

He told me about the shooting that December 14, 2012, where twenty-six people, twenty of whom were children died. The city of Newtown, Connecticut, chose to demolish the building. There are books, conspiracy theories, charities, lobbying group, and gun control laws about Sandy Hook. Again, the news was unsure about the killer's motivation, but his mother, the first one to die, had bought the guns for her son. And now those who own guns and who use them legally pay the price. Knee jerk laws chip away at the Second Amendment.

The First Amendment took a hit because some people filed lawsuits and won against those with differing outlooks and theories about the shooting. Massacres are like that. People try to reason how people could be so heartless. It is important to listen to all theories for fact finding and sorting out details if we are going to prevent evil from succeeding. Controlling the dialogue restricts truth from emerging. Justice can only be based on truth.

Franklin Regional High School, a few miles outside of the Pittsburgh city limits, hit the news during my work hours. A student took a knife and stabbed his schoolmates and one adult. Knives do not make as big a bang in the news as guns. No one died but at least two students were seriously injured. I was a temporary worker in a department, where, across the room, I could see one worker answering her cell phone, and pacing ... people with whom I worked had children attending the high school.

The parents of the knife-wielding student hired an attorney, rightfully so, to plead their son's case. Then several years later, they wanted to become advisors. They had missed the signs in their home—the kitchen knife was a clue—when the news hit the airwaves. The one thing they may be able to advise is missed warning signs. I met a PR team, two young people, who were hired to spin facts after the stabbings at Franklin Regional High School.

In Parkland, Florida, the high school was met with hate on Valentine's Day 2018. Some use the terms "MK Ultra" and "false flags" about massacres but those terms were used in this particular shooting. I am not sure of MK Ultra, but I said years ago that these students who are planning disasters are not doing it alone. They have to be talking to someone or they have to be triggered. What is triggering them? Well-planned shootings are not done at the hands of people who are ignorant of what they are doing. Of course, at the regional high school the police failed to go in right-away, which made matters worse. They found the shooter, who did not kill himself, at a restaurant nearby. He had warned he wanted to kill people. This school has become famous in the gun control lobbying efforts. But the gun is a weapon of choice: it is not the culprit.

CHAPTER 19

What set this student to kill? Did anyone watch his trial? How bad does it have to get to be called to testify at the murder trial of a student? A reenactment was done to determine the time delay in response. Using live ammunition, it was conducted as part of civil litigation. Some parents are using their forums to hold people accountable. Others, including one student, are trying to punish all who own guns.

While having breakfast at the kosher Jewish deli in the Oakland section of Pittsburgh (our Church Annex as we affectionately called it), we suddenly had the peace broken when patrons hurriedly answered text messages and phone calls. The men behind our table started to speculate about what was going down less than a mile away. I called my sister, who lived about two miles from the location, while the deli owner turned on the television for the news. A shooter had opened fire as he confronted the people in their synagogue at their Saturday morning services. Eleven people died. I attended a prayer service at The Soldiers and Sailors Museum, a political event with prayers and praise songs. People I knew lost a friend, colleague or neighbor that day. The shooter did get sentenced to death in the trial's penalty phase.

"Greg," a regular rider on P71, shared with me that he knew the student who opened fire from their high school in Olean, NY, many years earlier. I had never heard of it, just like the generation today may think Columbine is just a flower. Years put distance between an event and memories. Gun clubs were popular but only one student decided to shoot others. On December 30, 1974, in Olean, NY, a seventeen-year-old killed three people and injured eleven. Captured without being killed, the shooter killed himself in 1975 while in jail.

Not until I started to view movies of a new favorite actor did I learn of the Cokesville School Miracle. Prayer, they say, brought the victims through, alive. On May 16, 1986, two adults, one a deranged man, and his wife, entered a school and held the children and staff hostage to extort money. She accidentally detonated the bomb. He killed her and then killed himself, but all the hostages were rescued. Why is it that I did not remember that one either? This event was not a watershed event for me.

Interesting that these adults had brought bombs, weapons and a shopping cart into the school. A shopping cart going unnoticed? The mad bomber was not a stranger to the community either but was not a current resident. He used others in his plan, but they decided to report his plans to the authorities after arriving at the school. Rescue and recovery were enacted before anyone realized what was going on. Located in a rural area with a very small population, people select areas to reside in to be safe. One person can change the scope of life in a small community.

The school in Belsan (Russia) located where strife expected was under a politically motivated siege in 2004. The outcome of that hostage situation was not positive. I remember that day because it was the day Pipa and I passed in the hallway of our daughters' high school. How many schools in other nations get attacked without a blink here in the States unless a hot political topic is trending?

No geographical location is immune. It seems we are more shocked when tragedy presents in areas that appear tranquil, rural, or suburban and less shocked when violence is reported in Chicago or New York. The effects of violence are the same on the individuals in large cities, but the shock value does not register on the scale of "unbelievability" the same way as a massacre in "less likely to happen here" towns, cities, or countries.

The Penn State and the Church sexual abuse scandals clearly demonstrated the aftermath when messengers are afraid, not consistent, not believed or silenced. The cases show the legal responsibility, the lives injured or lost, and the financial cost, which can be insurmountable. Confidential settlements are problematic. School district personnel contributed to the silence in the Penn State and Church scandals.

Who is our neighbor?

REPLACEMENTS

Although the parents did not have a concern with the replacement for me in the classroom, my dismissal caused problems. Replacements in parenting also cause disruptions, problems, and sometimes lead to real tragedy.

As parents work more and get more involved with their activities, they leave their primary job to replacements or to "the wind." We see the changes in schools and culture. A young man of nineteen told me that his mother thought he could be on his own at the age of twelve. "She was wrong," he said. I met him in an at-risk youth program. He had already served time in juvenile detention. His mother spent a lot of money bailing him out of incarceration. It is said that it is easier to raise a child than to rehabilitate an adult. Some people miss parenting 101.

The song, *He's Got the Whole World in His Hands*[17] was changed to *We have the Whole World in Our Hands*. When I first heard that at a school concert sung by kindergarten children, I did think we had a reality problem here: how is it working out for us?

Raised in the late sixties and early seventies, I understood a woman has to be both a professional and a mom to be counted as doing something worthy. I lost status as a working woman in my mind and in the perception of others. I kept seeking guidance and praying that I would have a clear view in a new line of work. *The Wizard of Oz* from the 1939 movie kept playing over and over and over, and I asked God many times, "What do You want me to learn from the story?" Finally, I realized what Dorothy learned. Like her, I learned there is no place like home. It took me two years to figure that out. To truly have influence, I started with my family. Gleaning from researching the violent student on student attacks, minor or extreme, I could see how children fell through the cracks. Even in two parent families, when both are busy pursuing professional and personal interests, they leave their children to fend for themselves or to the caring or uncaring hands of others.

I stayed home for almost seven wonderful years, doing volunteer work at my church, in my children's schools, and with the local sports teams. I did not bring home a significant amount of bacon, but I did fry it up in a pan. My children said they did enjoy the time I was a stay-at-home mom, and so did I. I did not have to think about who would watch them if they got sick. I worked with a woman who told her kids if they were sick, "Throw up before 7:00 a.m." so she could call for a substitute.

In 2004, when I started looking for full time work, I was torn. My husband had decided on a plan in 2004 which had ripple effects. Split families can contribute to problems in the culture. I had to make sure my children kept their heads above water. I felt like Mary, living in a Martha's World. I wanted to continue to be a stay-at-home mother.

I wrote the following few thoughts and submitted them for publication to the local paper in 2004. Women do struggle with balancing the employed for pay status and being "just a mom." I had other editorials published on the subject but this one did not get accepted.

"I did not attend a workshop today because frankly, I could not afford it," said Mary, the woman who liked to listen to Jesus while her sister, Martha, who was doing much work, complained. Martha wanted Jesus to tell Mary to get to work. Once a Martha, working at home and as a teacher, I brought home a good income, took care of a household for my husband and me and later two children. I was also proud that I managed to fit in a lot of volunteer work on top of all that.

My children fit nicely into everything I wanted to do. I was dropping them off at the sitter's, school or before school care early. Sometimes I picked them at 6:00 p.m. My children loved their caregivers. My son complained that he was late at 7:15 a.m. His classes began at 9:00 a.m. As a mother, I did not realize that even though my children enjoyed their time, 10-hour workdays are hard on all bodies. Then bullets struck a school in Jonesboro as two disturbed students killed a colleague whom I had never met. As trouble continued to brew in my class, making my work environment unsafe, suddenly, I found myself no longer a Martha—at least as far as earning a paycheck.

I started listening to Jesus on a regular basis. I soon found that the Martha part of me, still viable, was turning more and more into a Mary, one who liked to listen to Jesus and His teachings. I found His way of life comforting.

Now the Mary part of me is being challenged to get a job, but the Martha in me says I am already working, I just do not get a paycheck. The Mary in me says stay close to Jesus. I hope to find an even balance somewhere in time.

I learned while being a Mary that children miss out when mom is constantly gone. There is no time to listen, neither to the children, nor to Jesus. The Mary in me says to remember to listen to Mary, the mother of Jesus. She was effective in this world, just being Mary, the mother of Jesus and the wife of Joseph, an exceptional man at any time.

My mom exemplified both a Mary and a Martha. Shannon Wright must have been a Mary and Martha too, and in her final moments of this earthly life, she did as Jesus did: "Greater love hath no one ..." I hope I meet her in heaven to tap her on the shoulder and say, "Thank you." A friend once gave me a printout of Jesus on the cross captioned: "I asked Jesus how much He loved me; then He stretched out His arms for me."

One of my favorite movies, *Courageous*, 2011 Tristar Pictures, focused on the father's role in the family. Released in 2011, it was produced by the Kendrick brothers as a Christian movie. The characters did not claim to be saints. The main character, the father of two children, got motivated when a drunk driver killed his daughter. It did not include dialogues about the evils of alcohol, changes to the drunk driving laws, and vengeance seeking. Instead, the man turned "to take the log out of his own eye" (Matthew 7:5). With devoted wives, the men vowed, in writing, their commitments to becoming better fathers. The producers intended the message to carry over into real-life with fathers pledging to do better.

Who will step up? The fathers each answered, "I will," and signed contracts/promises to be the men God created them to be.

Myth: Replacements can substitute for parents.

TAKING THE BLINDERS OFF—GUIDE TO SAFE SCHOOLS

It's been twenty-five years since I left the classroom, but some things never change. Statistics reported activists wanting fewer penalties when school violence was tracked (Pittsburgh Public Schools, June 26, 2023).

The continuum of violence at the extreme changes life for all. We teach to the abnormal and the special circumstances almost exclusively. A distortion of rights clouds education. Currently, for some, it is raining so hard the roofs are caving in. The frustration factor of students placed in learning situations beyond their capabilities strains them as well as our schools. Told to value our differences, at times we are doing the complete opposite: molding into one-size-fits-all hurts everyone. In my personal opinion, we shortchange the average and above average students as well as those who exhibit anti-social behaviors. Frustrations mount. Twenty-five years ago, my room was no exception.

In the *Guide to Safe School, Early Warning Timely Response* (Dwyer, Osher, Warger), experts from the educational field, principals, teachers, parents, and youth contributed to set out clear and uncluttered guidance. Intended to be distributed to all staff in every school across the country in the fall of 1998, the Guide hit the nail on the head in only thirty-two pages.

Richard W. Riley, Secretary U.S. Department of Education, and Janet Reno, Attorney General U.S. Department of Justice, introduced the *Guide* with these words:

America's schools are the safest places to be on a day-to-day basis, due to the strong commitment of educators, parents, and communities to their children. Nevertheless, last year's tragic and sudden acts of violence in our nation's schools remind us that no community can be complacent in its efforts to make its schools even safer.

There is a cautionary statement about making mountains out of molehills and "over reactions." Although it does not intend to label students, it states:

On June 13, after the tragic loss of life and injuries at Thurston High School in Springfield, Oregon, President Clinton directed the Department of Education and the Department of Justice to develop an early warning guide to reach troubled children quickly and effectively, This Guide responds to that Presidential direction. It is our sincere hope that this Guide will provide you with the practical help needed to keep every child in your school out of harm's way …

We know from research that children who become violent towards self or others feel rejected and psychologically victimized. In most cases, children exhibit aggressive behavior early in life and, if not provided support, will continue a progressive developmental pattern toward severe aggression or violence. However, research also shows that when children have a positive, meaningful connection to an adult, whether it be at home, in school, or in the community, the potential for violence is reduced significantly.

Tips for parents and students, teachers, administrators, and the community are listed in short paragraphs—no lesson plans, but a common-sense approach. "Do No Harm" listed first in the section titled: *Principles for Identifying the Early Warning Signs of*

Violence, starts with the proviso, "Not all behaviors lead to the extreme. Not every threat comes from within either."

Identifying and Responding to Imminent Warning Signs:

In situations where students present other threatening behaviors, parents should be informed immediately. School communities also have the responsibility to seek assistance from appropriate agencies.

Nowhere does it say this should be considered: that we turn in brother or sister, by falsely reporting.

Page 7 - Do No Harm:

Page 11 - Know The Law:

When we discern early signs in children, the message is clear. It is OK to be concerned when you notice warning signs in a child, and it is appropriate to do something.

Page 12 - Acknowledging the Child Is Troubled:

Everyone, including administrators, families, teachers, school staff, students, and community members, may find it too troubling sometimes to admit that a child close to them needs help. When faced with resistance or denial, school communities must persist to ensure that children get the help they need.

Page 13 - Effective Practices for Improving the Behavior of Troubled Children:

These practices are well documented in the research literature. Research has shown that effective interventions are culturally appropriate, family supported, individualized, coordinated, and monitored.

Shared Responsibility ideas recur throughout the thirty-two pages.

Page 31 - Conclusion:

School board policies must address both prevention and intervention for troubled children and youth. Procedures should encourage staff, parents, and students to share their concerns about children who exhibit early warning signs.

The title *Early Warning Signs* is a clear giveaway as to how one must act in a preventive manner. It does not mean calling 911 and waiting for the swat team. Intervention can be expensive; prevention on the other hand is less costly. I sought free, or at nominal cost, reports and guidebooks as I looked for evidence and affirmation for my response. I was not disappointed, nor, as I learned, was I alone. The findings were not shocking to those paying attention.

The experts involved in writing the Guide never recommended retaliation or denial, which are systemic problems and continue to influence decisions. Families deny abuse, corporations and government deny greed and corruption, school districts deny bullying, violence, and sexual assaults. We go back to the "ostrich whose head is stuck in the sand" scenario. But "What is done in the darkness will be exposed to the light," says 1 Corinthians 4:5. People do not think dark secrets will ever come out. The *Guide* helps to expose the darkness.

I met with Maurice Elias, a professor at Rutgers University, at the NJ Teachers' Convention in November 1998. Elias participated as an expert panel member for the *Guide* and presented at the convention. He listened as I shared my story, which I do not think shocked him in the least.

Once I learned the *Guide* existed, I ordered many free copies and gave them to parents, former colleagues, and other educators. The responses to my gesture were mixed. When I attempted to give one to a former coworker, whom I saw praying at Our Lady of Sorrows, he refused to take one and told me he did not care. I looked up at the Blessed Sacrament and told him, "He does!" Then I walked away.

The Press showed interest as they published my words:

If your school system does not admit there are problems in behavior within your system, find out what they are trying to hide ... Ask your local school district for a copy of *Early Warning Timely Response Guide to Safe Schools:* read it, share it, do it. An ounce of prevention is worth a pound of cure.

As we facilitated child assault prevention trainings, we memorized lines for the scenarios such as "the right to be safe and to feel safe." That bell curve of safety rings whenever the subject is people. Feeling, being, and functioning in the same environment can be different depending on the person but there is a general consensus as to what safe is.

Schools are safe, until they are not. I learned that as a high school student growing up during civil unrest and riots in my town. I generally felt safe in my high school, then one day it changed.

"Charge" yelled a student in my high school cafeteria as the riot began. I was sitting there when the staff told us to get to class as hell broke loose, not offering any guidance to leave the school. I saw bloodied heads of classmates and felt thankful that the group pushed me up the staircase and not down it. I was not afraid most of the time. I went back to school the next day.

500 students were afraid to go to school after a small group of suspended students ran through their high school in 2023. Their weapons were masks, hands and knowing how to manipulate the safety system. Other students allowed them in. No guns were reportedly used.

The New Jersey State Assembly Task Force on Adolescent Violence, June 1999, described several findings and recommendations similar to the problems I had experienced. My class was second grade, though the behaviors were more common in the adolescent age ranges. The findings indicated that teachers were getting wrongly disciplined for coming forward about violent behavior.

The over-zealous application of special education laws was found to be a factor in the discipline of violent children. Children with emotional problems often get a pass for hurting others because the experts say the actions are part of their disability. Are they? When they age out into adulthood, then commit crimes, their emotional mental health may be taken into consideration: but they still face legal accountability. Even pleading not guilty for reason of insanity does not keep one out of incarceration or a locked health institution.

There are many findings and conclusions in the report. Two findings pertinent to my situation were:

Page 2 #13:

Current law requires teachers to report acts of violence and vandalism to the Principal. Oftentimes, however, principals hesitate to report acts of violence to the district Superintendent due to the stigma that it attaches to the school and the fact that schools with a high rate of violence may not receive certain grants. Also, teachers who report acts of violence and vandalism received negative evaluations. Is the same attitude living and well?

Page 3 #15: The federal Disabilities Education Act and state special education regulations create a dual standard of discipline amongst students.

Line 8: According the report, New Jersey firearm statutes are among the strictest of any state in the nation. Current law prohibits a person from knowingly selling or transferring a firearm to a person under eighteen, and a violation of this law makes it a third-degree crime.

Line 28: According to testimony in the report received from the state Juvenile Justice Commission, severe punishment is not a deterrent to juvenile delinquency. Harsh penalties and extended sentencing may remove dysfunctional youth from the streets temporarily, but early detection of behavioral anomalies reduces and prevents youth delinquency and violence. The real goal focuses on rehabilitation to prevent future adult criminal activity.

Line 52 is about practice of a faith. It does not advocate formal religion in schools. I did not want my children evangelized either. Parents need to address what religion is appropriate for their children and family. The 1993 study was listed.

Line 52: According to a Brigham Young University study, family and religious influences may strongly deter delinquent behavior. The study found that those youth for whom religion was an important internal aspect of their lives resisted peer pressure and avoided delinquency to a greater extent than those youth who had not internalized gospel teachings. Contrary to previous research, religion made a significant contribution to predicting delinquency even in competition with peer and family influences (Chadwick, Bruce A and Top, Brent L *Religiosity and Delinquency among LDS adolescents*. Journal for the Scientific Study of Religion Volume 32 page 86, 1993).

> Suggestions in the report: Review current school policy of administering discipline to special education students pursuant to the Federal Individuals with Disabilities Act (IDEA) and review the impact of such provisions to prevent tipping the scales of justice in favor of juvenile offenders.
>
> Individual Educational Plans (IEP) are to specifically state the exemptions from discipline. If there are none, then the child is responsible for following all rules.
>
> Establish a school safety committee at each school to develop and implement a long-term action plan for violence intervention and crisis management with input from parents, school personnel and students.

In March 1998, The Learning Disabilities Teacher Consultant, the School Psychologist, and the social worker, who were part of the school's hurriedly put together safety team, submitted an unsigned letter against me. Although the Board was in possession of the letter, it was not in my file on the morning of April 20, 1998. Moreover, it was written before the assembly incident in which the troubled student stood up to "kill the umpire." Is the following unsigned letter an example of best practices when a teacher has concerns for the safety and well-being of the class?

Due to the nature of Mrs. Carlino's memo, this Child Study Team felt compelled to respond and clarify the issues raised about the child. Mrs. Carlino states that the child fits the profile of a child with potential to commit violent acts and further compares him to the children in Arkansas. At some point, there is no indication that this contention is true. In fact, there is evidence that his prognosis is hopeful. The parents have sought professional help. They are trying hard to make positive changes in his life. They have sought psychiatric consultation (2/27/97) and, as recommended, have placed their son on medication. His parents, in conjunction with the child study team and teachers, developed a special education program which includes learning resource center help for academics, and an intensive behavioral program designed by the school psychologist and implemented by his teachers, and parents. In addition, he receives weekly counseling by the school psychologist, who monitors his behavior via regular communication with his teachers. The school psychologist has been and remains available when the child requires additional help to control his behavior. He is showing progress in learning how to manage his anger and control his impulsiveness. Despite Mrs. Carlino's contention that the child has demonstrated minimal progress, since initial classification, there has been a significant reduction in aggressive behaviors, as documented by behavioral incident reports.

Mrs. Carlino, a certified special education teacher, has had multiple meetings with the school psychologist concerning this child's difficulties as well as training for her own special education certification. She was given books on oppositional defiance disorder, coached on how to talk to the child, and has ongoing contacts with the entire child study team as needed. She has been encouraged to seek additional training and consultation.

An aide was offered as an additional resource but was deemed not necessary by Mrs. Carlino, who felt his progress warranted no additional intervention. Regarding the family's personal issues, ongoing professional help was sought by the mother and the child. Unfortunately, Mrs. Carlino revealed details of a confidential meeting, which we feel could interfere with the relationship of trust that has been established with the family.

The administrative authorities are dealing with the staff member's indiscretion. As a child study team, we continue to remain sensitive to our students' needs, and confidentiality of information regarding students and their families, and hope to continue to have a trusting relationship with the parents. We oppose communications that needlessly label our students and reveal sensitive information carelessly.

Alluded to from a comment in the hearing, the letter was written to appease the parents as a rebuttal. While it does confirm the many steps taken, it left out the pivotal incident of March 24, 1998. The psychologist was the first one I contacted that day. She told me it would ruin her relationship with the child if she had to administer discipline. As for the professional counseling sought, the dates listed were for his first-grade year. No aide was continued from the first grade or offered for his second-grade year.

Is the rebuttal a good example of cooperation? If the child has seriously hurt someone, would a court see it as evidence? Why would the team want to undermine the teacher? The Learning Disabilities Consultant, the School Psychologist and the Social Worker did not sign the letter, but their typed names appeared with the date of 03/31/1998. Lawyers have since told me that I could have legally published in a newspaper, the workshop request concerns I had made to the administration and staff.

Myth: School district personnel have protected immunity from lawsuits.

1997-98 served as a dramatic wake-up call to the fact that guns come to school, and some students use them to kill. In spite of that, not everyone heard the bells ringing. The Child Study Team in my school put on the proverbial blinders and noise cancelling headsets.

We do not have to reinvent wheels; however, here is a reminder of how they spin. Violence is violence whether the weapon is a hand, a penis, a tongue, a knife, a bat, a desk, a chair, a gun, a truck, or a car. You can add to the list.

The Federal Education Rights and Privacy Act (FERPA) states that:

Educators are free to share information with other agencies or individuals about students based on their personal knowledge or observation, provided the information does not rely on the contents of an educational record. Oral referrals to other agencies based on personal observations are not subject to the provisions of FERPA.

Exceptions to the prior consent requirement: Is the disclosure being made to other school officials, including teachers, within the school or school district who have been determined to have legitimate educational interests? A school official has a legitimate interest if the official needs to review an educational record to fulfill his or her professional responsibility to officials of another school, school systems or postsecondary institution where the student seeks or intends to enroll.

Since the massacre at Virginia Tech, the FERPA regulations had been made clear as to sharing limitations. Educational institutions will not be fined or receive penalties for divulging information for prevention. The University of Colorado evidently did not read the information they were dealing with before their student carried out the massacre in the Aurora, Colorado movie theater.

Cho, the killer at Virginia Tech, who did not fit the media profile of mass shooters, had a history even in his middle and high school years. Was it only after the shootings that the records could be disclosed?

The Clery Act, named after a young woman who was raped and murdered on her college campus in Pennsylvania, mandates that colleges inform students about crimes on and around campus with timely responses to give students and staff ample warning to protect themselves. The learning can be curvy. On my small campus in the 1970s an intruder entered a building with a controlled access door and raped a female student. This was before the Clery Act. We found out by word of mouth.

The Clery Act was updated after the Virginia Tech massacre. Virginia Tech violated clauses that mandate warning students of dangers on post-secondary educational campuses. The catch 22 is that children who are violent get classified for funding reasons early on and it gets harder to share when they become adults. Special education laws involve money. Fear of financial penalties comes into play with laws such as the Clery Act, FERPA, as well as the Individuals with Disabilities and Education Act. Violations can be costly but so can the interpretations.

At the community college where I worked with at-risk youth and also in a federally funded ESL program, I disagreed with a presenter who was explaining the American with Disabilities Act about the reasons for staff not being informed when plans needed to be adapted. She called me paranoid. A college employee was severely injured on campus not long after. The staff member was well liked.

In the fall of 2023, the University of Pittsburgh in Pennsylvania installed panic buttons in classrooms. The campus experienced false alarms earlier that year about active shooters. The campus is close to the synagogue that did have an active shooter in 2018. On August 28, 2023, a Chinese graduate student shot and killed his professor at the University of North Carolina at Chapel Hill, as a result of which the college went into lockdown. Morgan State University made national news with the mass shooting on October 13, 2023, for which a seventeen-year-old has been arrested.

I sat in court, listening in on an appeal hearing for someone who is on death row. He had been accused and found guilty in a judge trial (not a jury trial) of murder. His WRAT (Wide Range Achievement Test) scores from his early elementary years together with his elementary school records were entered in as evidence to show long term problems, traced back to his early development including asking questions of the circumstances at birth and other records. Mitigating circumstances did not change the sentence, even though the appeal hearing judge had his feet up on the bench the entire time.

Early on in my research, I came across the work of Gavin De Becker, a world-renowned security expert. I bought his book *The Gift of Fear*,[18] read it, highlighted it, and purchased copies for distribution. My son's third grade teacher, who was then the local association President of our community's school district, was the only one who would not accept one. It was not a dangerous read. Gut feelings are real: intuition is our gift of fear. Both are gifts from God. Not one teacher in my children's school offered me any words of comfort or assistance except for the Community and Recreation Director. His kind words meant so much. Shunning by one teacher in particular was visible.

Several years later, when I presented a few training sessions, my audiences were mostly teachers. Some were very interested, others not so much. In the workshops that I led, I presented facts and earned about $300 per workshop. I did not try to further my career or to become a keynote comedian. I used the following from the Gavin De Becker Inc. website, as an example:

A teacher posed a question in his chat. The teacher described a child's artwork that showed very graphic attacks on students and teachers. Per the comment, the child had homicidal ideations. The questioner had consulted the teacher from the child's previous year. They both agreed that the student exhibited the most aggressive and disruptive behaviors of all those with whom they had ever worked. Neither the school social worker nor the mother of the child expressed concern when this teacher informed them.

This chat comment resonated with me.

I had given a story booklet to the psychologist which two boys and this student had worked on together. With guns (no roses), police, and parent characters, the boys created an action story. Children do play with toy guns, play cops and robbers, and have fantasy play acting. Lines drawn, the history of behaviors counts. I wanted someone else on the team to see it.

This is a direct quote from Gavin De Becker in response to a question:

Indeed, it is a serious matter, and your personal challenge appears to be that people are not listening. Whenever that is the case, I propose changing the medium. Switch to writing your concerns in a letter to your Principal and/or Superintendent. You might include text along these lines: "Chronically angry children need intervention beyond what I can offer in the classroom if I am to meet my obligation to the other students. I am concerned about the boy's welfare and the safety and well-being of students around him for the following reasons (your list).

For more information: https://gdba.com/child-safety/#questions-for-your-childs-school Before I read that a security expert recommended the action, I had already submitted my list on March 25, 1998. An expert was once a beginner. Wearing blinders does not help in preventing violence.

Myth: People who follow their gut reactions live in fear.

HANDLING STORMY WEATHER AT HOME, WORK AND PLAY

On September 5, 1980, a call to the office came in for me and I had to go to the office to answer it. It was my sister on the line. I asked if my mom was OK. Then the words came that my beautiful, red-haired, sweet, bright five-year-old niece had died. She had been sick with a virus for a short time but was immune compromised because of a healing heart condition. Fellow staff members heard me scream. Of all the deaths of people in my family, my niece's has been the hardest. I did look back that week and was comforted when I saw that we did have Christmas in July and a Thanksgiving dinner on the Labor Day weekend before she died. She went to her first and only day of kindergarten and was dead less than two days later. Her animal is the rabbit, a symbol of God.

"A rabbit once did guard my door, to give me strength forever more to know that from the heavens above, we are looked upon by eyes of love." This was our Christmas card in 1980 remembering the rabbit that was sitting in front of our front door when we left for the funeral. The best way I cope in times of utter sadness is turning to God and crying out to Him for answers. How do you deal with a child's death? Does your heart break also?

Her parents gave me a mustard seed necklace when I was in junior high. I had to have "faith the size of a mustard seed." I had been experiencing vertigo spells after her death and before my mom died just eleven months later, on August 6, 1981. I was 26 then, feeling too young to have lost my mom. My vertigo spells never came back after she died. Did she put a word in for me? The monarch butterflies, on their migration path, were in our area when she died. Butterflies, resurrection symbols, brought comfort. That is one reason why my second grade was named Beautiful Butterflies, for my first teacher of faith.

My favorite scene of any movie is from *Terms of Endearment*, 1983 Paramount Pictures, in which Shirley McClaine plays the mother of a woman who is in the final stages of cancer. The mother slams her hands on the nurse's station and yells at them to give her daughter medication for the pain. Another favorite scene is when the mother is in the car on the beach with the character played by Jack Nicholson. The "bug up your ass" line should not be "killed with alcohol." When I have "a bug up my bonnet," something is wrong. What sets your senses off?

Animals can sense danger. When a dog barks, do you tell it to shut up or go look to see why the dog is on alert? Gut feelings can clue a child to hold off the creepy person who is intent on assault. If a child does not like someone, that could be a warning sign. Do not make your child "dance for grandma." We do not want them to be rude but giving them authority over their bodies is empowering them to stay safe. Children are perceptive about other children also. Pay attention if your child does not like another child.

Myth: If you can't say something nice, don't say anything at all.

What do we have in our homes now that did not exist before the seventies? My oldest brother, working for a company that entered the market early, was ahead of the curve promoting smoke detectors. People thought he was nuts. As a weatherman for the Air Force, he always paid attention to the weather too. Who has a weather app on their phone? It is now mandatory to have smoke and carbon dioxide detectors.

For eight years, I resided in an ocean community. Tides and water levels matter for those who live at or below sea level. We lived half a block from the wetlands to the left, with the bay a few blocks behind us. The ocean waves lapped at the beach about five blocks in front of us. To get to work, we had to travel a few miles up the island. Strong storms could be a threat, and we had several in my thirty-five years of living on an island or in a community surrounded by bay water. The one that did the most damage for us was a Nor'easter which required moving our cars. One morning I woke up at 5:30 to no rain, no water but by 6:30, water was above the wheel wells. We did not make that mistake again. I also lived in the region of New Jersey, just south of where the eye of Hurricane Sandy hit. I invited a woman, who lived in a vulnerable area, to stay with me the day before the storm. Her living quarters were destroyed; the people who did not evacuate had to be rescued.

Storms are not always waterlogged. Wind, sand and people can create worse storms than any rainstorm. The Bible tells of seeing the clouds in the sky and to prepare; but we do not see the signs of the times. History repeats itself, and so must I.

After an emotional storm, exhaustion can set in. After a rampage, witnesses speak of the calm perpetrator. Anger can be motivating if righteous, while vengeful anger seeks to destroy. How do you feel after a rant? How do you feel when your motivation is for positive change or results?

Community violence and workplace versus school violence: Is there a difference? What would you tolerate in your community or corporate site?

I lived in Pittsburgh in 2020, the "Summer of Love." The one riot and many protests were handled well considering the destruction in other cities. I did take myself to city hall the day after the riot. Sticks, stones, bricks, looting and setting fires, but no one used gunfire that weekend, although guns were clearly visible. Not every store in downtown was damaged, but the CVS, a clothing store, a Starbucks, Footlocker and several other small stores were destroyed. The looters left nothing, and all the windows were broken. I could not go into my work building on the next workday because someone had left a bookbag of homemade "cocktails" near the headquarters of a major national company.

The police did find the person who allegedly left it. But I did witness the good in people at 6:00 a.m. the next morning in volunteer and paid clean-up crews who started at 3:00 a.m.

Protesting went on all summer and into the fall. One demonstration, which involved restaurants and beer, made national news. I surveyed many with my Rosary beads in hand. The crowds yelled provocative and threatening chants, wore military type uniforms and wore dark masks covering all but their eyes—and not because of Covid. I discussed with business leaders that the city in which I was raised never returned to normal after the riots in the 60s.

Violence does not have to be physically destructive. How many false alarm fire drills are we to tolerate before we say something? How many would you accept at your workspace? A thirteen-year-old and an eleven-year-old excused themselves from class, pulled a fire alarm, then killed five people at Shannon's workplace.

The Press of Atlantic City, December 10, 2003

Recently, HS has had several false alarms. Having gone to high school and worked in schools myself, I am familiar with the drill. As a student, one usually takes the event in one's stride. As a teacher, one often gets used to the distraction. That is where the problem is. False alarms, whether caused by pulled handles, smoking or highly sensitive systems that react to dust, should never be taken as the standard operating procedure.

Disrupted classes, invalidated tests, delayed performances, standing out in cold weather in swim trunks, none of that is life threatening (well maybe the last one is.) However, at each alarm, the fire company must come out and inspect; so, must the police. Could there be a mundane reaction to a real fire? What if a real-life fire started while the limited manpower is busy at a false alarm? False alarms are costly, and, yes, are a punishable offense. But here is the rub. How many offenders do it because false alarms in school seem to be a rite of passage?

The fire department was called to the high school on the opening night of a drama club production. Not a scheduled drill, and no one caught? Years later, I was told that an alarm was pulled while the PSATs, used to determine Merit Scholarships, were being administered. The participant told me years later, not one adult said anything. Teachers monitor those standardized tests.

Do you remember when college campuses were having regular disruptions due to fire alarms and bomb threats called in through technology that disguised the caller's location? I do; my daughter's college campus was a victim. Sirens and fire drills at 2:00 a.m. are alarming. We have seen a high-level government official pull an alarm in the Capitol building. Why? Could it be for distraction? Old techniques work for criminals.

Employers have obligations to their employees for safety. OSHA rules, compliance, human resources either mandate or follow mandates. Law departments make up a large part of corporate America. Why? Did we learn anything in the last several years? Do politicians care? Do leaders in business follow the money? Do education associations look after the best interests of the children or families? Recall the lockdowns, masks on young children, and remote learning.

New Jersey State Statutes mandate safe schools reporting any incidents and have protections for reporters in the School Safety Act of 1982. Every state has laws with websites discussing problems and solutions. Associations address their views on their websites. Incident forms or FYI forms, personal notes, documents, "Write down the vision, clearly upon the tablet."

Some mandates are meant to protect. Others are meant to harm. The more we let the extremes dictate how we live our lives, the more we are unsafe and not free. The extremes can kill us or our spirits. How do trainers break an animal?

All staff must be involved: if there is a pecking order, you will have problems. Secretaries, maintenance staff, cafeteria workers, volunteers, bus drivers should have a voice. Twenty-five years ago, these staff members were excluded. Misbehavior on the school bus is well documented in news events. Often, misbehaving students sat in the office keeping the secretary company. The secretaries took the threatening phone calls or bomb threats. One retired secretary made decisions to evacuate or stay inside. That may not have been a bad idea but was it just years of experience or her gut reaction leading to discern what to do? The association President wrote about that scenario after Columbine.

The cumulative effects of small incidents can equal any major event. Minor instances may be precursors of future large-scale events. Criminals test vulnerabilities. An abused person is usually not killed on the first assault. But lines are crossed little by little, and sometimes the abusive or violent behaviors are unrecognizable at first.

How many times have we heard those culprits are just boys being boys? I completely agree that boys and girls are different. With gender identity a sensitive topic, how would you explain violence today? How do you explain it when a woman kills?

Violence, a societal problem becomes a school problem when people manifest violent behaviors on the grounds, from the grounds, on a bus or in the hallways. The first step in foiling a crisis is recognizing and accepting the fact that every school—every classroom—has a certain degree of risk. Unsafe schools are not effective learning environments. Not all children demonstrate resiliency. Learn the difference between prevention, intervention, rescue and recovery.

For a group of teachers in an inner-city school, I found an ad from Merck Chemical, the Vaccination Division, with a copyright date of 1998. The teddy bear toy in the picture had one tear, which may have been a throwback reminder to the tearful Native American in ads years before. I used the ad to compare statistics in seeking solutions.

The ad's words were all in capital letters:

TRAGICALLY, ABOUT FORTY CHILDREN DIE EACH YEAR BECAUSE OF PROBLEMS DUE TO CHICKENPOX. AND, SADLY, NEARLY 7,300 KIDS END UP IN HOSPITAL. HELP

PROTECT YOUR CHILD AGAINST CHICKENPOX. ASK YOUR DOCTOR HOW.

Do you mandate a new medication on the population due to forty deaths a year? It seems we do. In my years of teaching and working with children, only one child had temporary neurological side effects from chicken pox. She went on to compete in ice skating competitions.

Does everyone take a dose of medication to stay healthy? Individualized Education Plans, meant to be for the individual, may be imposed unnecessarily on everyone in the class. The majority of gun owners do not commit crimes; most kitchen knives are used to cut food. Are you waiting for mandates on who owns knives?

Prayer became my way of life. I thought after a few months I would feel good enough to not want to attend daily Mass or spend time in Adoration. I was wrong. I did feel better as prayer and Mass became part of my daily walk. Sometimes we fall into routines out of habit. That was not the case for me. I began noticing other new people at daily Mass. How did others arrive at this point? A few times I saw people who never attended Mass, sitting in the church praying. Praying in Mass daily, when we are burdened, soon turns into thankfulness, with those two emotions sometimes switching back and forth.

At the old school, a group of parents would bring us treats for the morning, just for the teachers. They were a prayer group who "adopted" us.

The Atlantic City Press August 12, 1999, Bless the Children and Schools

Much to the delight of many parents and the disappointment of many children, the beginning of a new school year will soon be upon us. Preparations are underway, buying new clothes, shoes, bookbags and other supplies. Each year brings a new level of anticipation, excitement and anxiety. We need to prepare our children for these. There are several ways to do this orientation:

visits to the new class or building and contacting school district personnel. Don't be afraid to ask questions. Back to school means preparing our children to work within group settings in an equitable way. Parents try to remember what is like two weeks into the summer when the novelty of being home has worn off and siblings begin to bicker. Multiply that by 25 or so different personalities and you might have more empathy for the teacher after the first few weeks of school.

We need to remember that in many aspects of our lives, marriage, birth anniversaries and deaths, we asked for blessings on new beginnings and endings. It is not an impossible test to ask as far as children are concerned as they go off to school.

We have a separation of church and state in this country to prevent one dominant denomination from controlling another (aka the government). In this way, we do not suffer separation from our individual right to practice religion and faith in God.

So, as we prepare our children for another school year, let us not forget to ask for blessings for our children as they enter upon a new journey. Let's do a collective prayer and ask that our schools will be safe havens for all the people who play and work in them.

The editor added a qualifier, "Marian Carlino is a former teacher."

I was not the only one practicing my faith. I would see the aide from my class at the chapel for Mass. The first-grade teacher often attended Mass at my church. At one prayer service, several years later, the school social worker was in my church. We did speak. And without us ever saying a word to each other, there was some sort of connection between a local psychologist and me. I saw him and his wife frequently at Sunday Mass through the years. He, I was told, was called in after I had left the classroom. I was never sure whether he was the crisis counselor.

Myth: Prayer is a useless activity.

ADVOCACY

1997-98 began with the death of Eddie Werner, a six-year-old boy from a town not far from where I lived. Eddie had been selling items door-to-door for a fundraiser when he was murdered. The murder made national headlines because of Eddie's age, the activity in which he was engaged when he was killed, and his murderer's age. The killer, Sam Manzie, Eddie's neighbor, was an emotionally disturbed teenager and a victim of abuse. The murder put the spotlight on sexual predators, the internet, and children going door-to-door for fundraising and changed the course of fundraising in schools and community organizations across the nation. Policies no longer allowed door-to-door solicitations. The conversation about abusers also opened the door to discuss safety on the internet because Sam Manzie's abuser contacted him through chat rooms. The two families suffered greatly but their faith practices and belief in forgiveness led them to national television to show their common bond. Both families recognized that they had both lost their children.

What motivates you to take a stand or protect someone else?

On October 8, 1997, Pipa came to my door and told me one student from my class had to leave with her. She took the student with no explanation. Fortunately, as noted earlier, in a small school people can communicate. While Pipa never did explain the absence, the coworker who did notify the authorities, informed me. The home environment was not safe. A child in the home reported the abuse despite the threats he had received. The young girl and her brave young relative are heroes, but not the adults who were living in the household. The girl in question did not smile in most pictures and on the day she was removed from my class, she wanted to stand rather than sit at her desk. It was not her typical daily behavior. I was heartsick.

Did the teacher, nurse and secretary miss signs of abuse when she was in first grade? There was discussion. The secretary said the mother was as sly as a fox. Were the marks cigarette burns? The kids too asked, "When is she coming back?" I could not answer that question for them, but I did keep her desk in place until February.

Years later, I learned that, since sexual assaults hurt, a child may be uncomfortable sitting. I ran a class in which the children could stand even when I was teaching as long as the view of another child in large group instruction was not blocked. Students could go to the bathroom without a lot of fanfare. We had a bathroom in the old room, and I had the room across from the lavatory in the new school, so I could see who was leaving.

Teachers learn a lot from their students. That pictures tell a thousand words rings true. Without reading more into them, it may be that a child who never smiles in pictures is hiding a truth. Had I missed two signs? Third party reporting is difficult when trying to secure intervention for a family. I do ask God for signs, affirmations and confirmations. It is not because I mistrust God; it is because I do not always get things right. I did get a chance to see the girl at my church.

In December 2004, I was hired to work at the local community college, in a grant funded program with at-risk youth. This was not my first rodeo working with youth who have fallen through the cracks. Teen pregnancy, drugs, delinquency, jail time, family dynamics and family income factored in for clients' eligibility. I was their job coach and advocate.

I took training to work in a formal child assault prevention program in the summer of 2005. It was an international endeavor, with state and county leaders. Teaching techniques of intervention was a priority. I was already working with young adults who were catching up. I became a facilitator, doing role play and discussions in participating schools from kindergarten through eighth grade. As adults, we memorized scenarios and the narratives—same page, same message, without personal interjections. Many of my coworkers were retired teachers and parents. My county leader had no formal training but was dynamic. We role played scenarios about bullying as well as physical and sexual abuse. Each scenario was developmentally appropriate for the grade level and at least two facilitators led each one. I led many scenarios for the eighth-grade boys. Does the Jerry Sandusky/Penn States' scandal ring another bell curve? Who were the victims?

Participation for students was voluntary. Parents could sign their children out of classroom presentations if they considered the subject matter was not appropriate. Participants could opt to speak to us individually about the scenarios. Most just wanted to chat, but if a child disclosed anything that would be considered a reportable offense, we became "mandated reporters." We had to contact the authorities, and then the authority may or may not further investigate the report. I even facilitated in my former district.

In sexually abusive situations, the elephant in the room is power and control. One would not meet with your rapist to resolve the abuse. Peer mediation and meeting with the person who is bullying is also counterproductive and dangerous. The words NO and STOP have to be understood. If we do not stop violence in its seedling stage, it festers and grows. Adults, social service agencies and lawyers may step in, not always successfully.

On one occasion in early 2008, another facilitator had to make a report. However, the program administrators violated their policy and answered a call from a father after this facilitator made the report. We were usually at a school for a few days to cover all participating classes. One day we were told we could not leave due to that conversation. Then we found out that a new policy under the agency was being instituted which required facilitators to obtain permission from the local county coordinator to report. This new policy violated the mandated reporters' law.

Years before that, when teachers reported, they had to go to the administrator first. You can imagine how that worked. Now this program was back tracking and breaking state law. I told the county coordinator I would walk outside and report. She told me anyone who did report without permission, would be fired. I told her to take my name off the roster until they had a legal review. The state leaders told me they thought I had been easy to work with, until then. Nevertheless, I contacted the county's prosecutor's office and the Diocese since the Catholic Church had contracted with the private agency to run the program. I was dismayed at the agency's attempt to silence the facilitators and their disregard for the law. This time the prosecutor's office and the Diocese paid attention, and the agency had to rethink their new policy. My fellow facilitators thought the policy for permission to report was not legal or right, but they continued to work without question. I officially resigned from the program, no longer trusting their judgment.

The jury is out on the effectiveness of state-run programs to protect abused children. The failure rate of government agencies is debated and documented. Trusted adults are not always family members, teachers, clergy, community emergency helpers or case workers, and private charities have a dark history. However, doing nothing is not an option. Reporters are there to tell the situation, and state agencies to investigate.

And children have intuition. They should be trained or be allowed to use it. Trust in the words of a child; it can be shocking as to the who, what, where, when and why of abuse. It may be a stranger who puts a child in danger, but more than likely it is a familiar person. The pattern of grooming is predictable. It could be a stranger who sees something is wrong, and acts.

New Jersey laws were clear about reporting child abuse. Anyone eighteen or older who suspects abuse is mandated to report. Here's an excerpt:

Failure to report can jeopardize the health and well-being of a child, and there are penalties for not reporting. Physical injury by other than accidental means, causing substantial risk of death or serious disfigurement or protracted impairment of physical or emotional health; sexual abuse or acts of sexual abuse; willful abandonment; willful isolation of ordinary social contact to indicate emotional or social deprivation; inappropriate placement in an institution; neglect by not supplying adequate care, necessities, or supervision.

The Penn State and the Church abuse scandals are prime examples of legal charges when abuse is not reported and/or covered up.

Again, the line between victims and perpetrators can be a fine one. I was searching the Megan's Law website frequently to see if a former neighbor was on the list. I searched by alphabetical order and saw the name of one adult male. He had been a student of mine in one of my first-grade classes in the early 1980s. My heart sank. This man, as a young child had learning challenges, a difficult family, and possible health issues. His LRC teacher was very rough on him one day about a bowel accident. Teachers were not trained in any warning signs of abuse in the past. Could it have been a sign we missed?

Unlike Mr. Roger's Neighborhood, not everyone is good, nor is every neighbor a good person. In the very early 60s, when I was in early elementary school, my mom reported a man who would stand at the corner in front of a neighbor's house. He would have the girls do somersaults—dresses were the fashion, not pants. He did serve time, but we saw him drive by in his blue car not long after. When my children were in middle and high school, once we learned what he was doing, the direction was to call 911 if they ever saw a man we knew on our street.

White picket fences do not guarantee goodness. I found my neighbor's name on the site, not for what he did in my neighborhood, but for what he had done in another town—another person, who got away with behaviors clearly indicative of an abuser.

A neighbor asked me one day if I'd heard what was happening on our street. Further discussion led to a revelation that involved a phone call to the police. The perpetrator drank and did not have a good reputation. Eventually his name made it to Megan's List—but not before he hurt a child in another part of the state and molested or tried to molest people in my neighborhood. He used a video machine in a neighbor's home, with her permission. When she walked into her living room from outside, he was masturbating. A single, adult woman, she did not call the police. He ran naked around the house across the street from me. He called the woman's name, and she found his clothes in her yard. She called the police but did not identify him. To yet another neighbor, he called asking for help. The woman sent her granddaughter. The girl ran from the house because he came out of the bathroom with just a towel on, trying to get her to the basement. The grandmother did not call the police either. Before these incidents, he would show up drunk at another neighbor's house.

This man lived with his grandmother off and on as well as in another city. He worked for a small electrical business, the type of business which sends workers into homes for small jobs. It is against the law to target Megan's List dwellers.

Besides proximity, a common factor that the people shared was living alone or the husbands working at night. Perpetrators do target their victims, while a victim's silence is a great advantage to the abuser. In our meeting with the police, one person documented in a letter, a former neighbor gave permission to tell her story and the other two women met at my house with the police officer who was also a friend and community member. "We know all about ..." was the policeman's comment.

Besides rejection, once one starts discussing the sexually explicit topics, people start to open up. I should not have been, but I was surprised, when three elderly people told me their abuse history. One had a very astute mother who had the father put in jail due to child abuse. Another one looked down at the ground and said, "May he rest in peace." Two other women who shared their stories never reported their abusers who were still living. People forget that forgiveness does not exclude justice.

Thumper's Daddy was wrong.

The advice by Thumper's daddy to the little rabbit, in the Disney movie, *Bambi* about not saying anything unless it is nice is totally ill advised. It may not be nice subject matter telling an adult that someone is abusive. In fact, it could bring about a firestorm of controversy and trouble for the victim. But saying something, although it may not be nice, must be told for the abuse to stop.

Since I had so much difficulty obtaining the minutes, when the news ran articles about a revision to the Open Public Records law, I contacted my representatives. Civil authorities were making it difficult to obtain public records, so I told my story to the local newspaper.

Atlantic City Press, August 1, 2001, Public Access Law Will Help Us All
     If we had friends in high level government positions, we would not have to worry about the lack of good access laws. We would just have to make a few phone calls. But that is not the case for the majority, who may have to wait for weeks or months to get what they are looking for, if they get it at all. That is why the public should pay attention to the problems regular citizens have in getting access to public information due to stonewalling or ignorance by government employees ... we will all benefit from the bill that is languishing in the assembly.

The legislature passed the bill, and one year later I wrote: "The government records council is an important aspect of legislation ... This law may not be perfect, but it is a start."
     News outlets and organizations have had to file lawsuits to get records for the March 27, 2023, killings at the Covenant School in Nashville, Tennessee. The female shooter, self-identified as a male, blasted her way in, leaving a manifesto. Different groups have motivations to disclose or not to disclose the rants of a murderer. An active investigation is currently ongoing. I wonder why we want to obtain the writings of a killer? How will

the manifestos be used? Is a killer insane before or just after the detailed plans are executed?

I wrote to representatives for changes in the anti-bullying laws when they came up for discussion in the state legislature. Implementation can make or break the meaning of a law leading to disconnections. A researcher, Dan Olweus, became a popular term in education after April 20, 1999.

The Current published:

Several years ago, a researcher in the field of bullying did a study in Norway and Sweden (1973) after there were a number of suicides blamed on bullying. His name is Dan Olweus[19]. He developed a list of signs which included physical, verbal, emotional, racist, and sexual behaviors. Persistent bullying can result in depression, low self-esteem, shyness, poor academic performance, isolation, threatened or attempted suicide …

Preventing bullying is a now a legal responsibility. There have been many cases in which district personnel have been held legally responsible for not upholding the discipline rules of the laws of our state. Those found negligent lost increments and jobs. There is no excuse not to enforce the anti-bullying laws. These are protections for those who do their jobs in preventing any type of violence or bullying.

The following is a quote from *Psychology Today* September/October 1995.

It is a blow to the very soul of freedom. Bullying violates fundamental democratic principles. If two kids were merely challenging each other, they would fight fairly; one would win and the other would lose, they would shake hands, and that would be the end of that. But the problem is that bullies seek out the victims and persecute them. They follow them and wait for them to harass them. It is a basic democratic right for a child to feel safe in school and to be spared the oppression and repeated, intentional humiliation implied in bullying.

Young bullies, female and male, grow into adult bullies if they are not stopped. So, prevention, not only benefits the initial victims, but the bullies themselves.

Dan Olweus' techniques have been used extensively.

Olweus died in 2020. https://olweus.sites.clemson.edu/history .php#:~:text=For%20approximately%2040%20years%2C%20 Dan%20Olweus,the%20Netherlands%2C%20the%20 USA%2C%20and%20Norway.&text=For%20approxi- mately%2040%20years%2C,the%20USA%2C%20and%20 Norway.&text=40%20years%2C%20Dan%20Olweus,the%20 Netherlands%2C%20the%20USA%2C.

We have heard the Jerry Sandusky excuse of just "horsing around" in the showers. We also hear the words, "just joking," and "prank." But some behaviors are actually physical assaults and illegal. "Take it for the team," they say. Well, no one has to take any type of assault for any team. Hazing is a criminal offense. Prevention is defensive; assaults are offensive.

In September 2023 according to news reports on several web- sites, the family of a young boy killed in an incident categorized as bullying has received a settlement from a school district in California for $27 million. It is a record-breaking financial set- tlement. The two boys who killed him were charged in juvenile court with involuntary manslaughter and did serve limited time. A principal and two assistant principals lost their jobs. The parents' complaints and concerns were inadequately addressed. It took four years for the settlement to be reached. We put price tags on life, when really a life is priceless. At least two boys and three adults did not get it.

For a list of jury settlements a summary as of December 2017 is listed in Public Justice Impact Change: https://www .publicjustice.net/wp-content/uploads/2018/01/2018.01.08- Winter-2017-Edition-Bullying-Verdicts-and-Settlements -Final.p

One would think that I would be a death penalty proponent. But one of my issues when I left teaching was the violation of my rights. Theoretically, I had a whole association to protect me, but corruption runs in all areas of life, including the court system. When the debate came up for change in NJ in 2002, I shared my story to my representatives and later met two women who were directly impacted in my own small community. The mothers strengthened my resolve for prevention. Perspective is everything.

The man who was convicted in NJ was executed, protesting his innocence until his death. He was not on death row for very long. The other murders in 2005 took place in Pennsylvania. Solitary confinement, one hour a day out of the cell, restrictions and only approved visitors is not living the good life. I made trips to the prison and waited as my friend entered through the many gates.

My faith strengthened me to continue to speak up for the unborn. I had already been active in church prolife activities and became more involved after I left teaching. If we consider the innocent, the unborn are the most oppressed. The most egregious form of violence is legal and befalls the most vulnerable in a place that should be the safest place in the world. Sharp medical instruments are the weapons of choice. Connecting dots, abortion sends a clear message to everyone that if there is a problem, it is acceptable to kill it. Abortion on demand is celebrated. A presidential candidate in 2016 introduced her choice to run for V.P. in front of Planned Parenthood.

N.J. Governor, Tom Kane, mandated, after his tour of concentration camps in Europe, that developmentally appropriate material on the Holocaust should become part of the curriculum from kindergarten to 12th grade. A N.J. college department led a workshop on Holocaust studies. The presenter told me, in response to my question, that, ironically, they did not discuss abortion in the syllabus.

This was the editorial to which Pipa referred when I questioned the move to the new school. I do believe this editorial can be heard in my rebuttal and workshop request.

Pro-life The Atlantic City Press February 1998

I hope this letter is redundant because we remember and learn through repetition. I recently attended a workshop on the mandated teaching of the Holocaust/ genocide curriculum in the New Jersey public schools. I hope, after reading this, that at least one other person learns the same powerful lesson that I did. I heard once again that prejudice and murder are wrong and that these are crimes against humanity. I knew that, but I what I also heard pulled hard at another part of my heart: the part that abortion is wrong.

I heard that we can make no comparison between the crimes of the Holocaust and abortion. Holocaust targeted specific groups of people for annihilation. And, yet, coming out of that workshop, I learned that we should make comparisons. I learned that I have to do more than just have a personal view that abortion is wrong. I learned that I have to become a vocal voice against abortion, and not just in my small circle of friends or at church. And, if I do not speak out, more innocent victims would be killed. And then, I have learned nothing from the teaching. Reasons for abortion are based on the same reasoning of the Nazis. It was specifically pointed out that the handicapped were the first to be murdered. It was the educated among them, doctors and nurses, who made those decisions. I heard once again that the victims were killed against their free will. I heard once again that the Nazis were not crazy; they had a plan. I heard once again that millions of innocents died. So, I will repeat that abortion kills the truly innocent among us and it is with a plan. I can no longer be silent. My silence makes me no better than anyone else who sends innocent people to their deaths. Who among us can afford to be silent?

I bought *Bella*, 2006, Metanoia Films, a prolife movie, in DVD format to give to people. While standing in the vestibule of my church, I asked a man who was standing there if he had seen it. He said no, but that his granddaughter's name was Bella. He took the DVD I offered him. The male lead in the movie, Bella, is the producer and plays the millionaire who funds the sting operation in

Sounds of Freedom, 2023, Metanoia Sante Fe Films. *Sounds of Freedom* is about human trafficking. Saving children is a common bond.

I joined one March for Life in 2014. The group I was with did not march to the Supreme Court. After standing in the bitter cold and listening to the speakers, my group instead prayed at the Basilica. I did street advocacy because there is a very lucrative abortion clinic in my city. I managed and wrote for a local organization's prolife blog for several years. Assaults on witnesses and prayers have been escalating in recent years. Eventually, as the interferences increased from verbal to physical, security guards and cameras became the norm.

Divorce can be a factor in children's behavior. Sadly, two families were going through theirs in 1998, but neither family wanted to notify us. The two children did not act out and seemed to be handling the changes in their homes but telling us would have been warranted. Divorce divides and conquers just like violence does and children become more vulnerable.

I informed my children's teacher and their friends' parents about my own divorce. Their Superintendent came to morning Mass regularly. He also took my calls or saw me when I asked.

I wrote a few editorials and contacted my state representatives when changes in NJ divorce laws were being discussed. A priest and a lawyer told me that I could not force someone to stay married. In 2005, "No Fault" grounds made the process uglier than it needed to be.

Some may say that "No Fault" increased the rate of divorce. That may be true. It is a dangerous time in a family's life. Making up charges to get out fast, one would think, would be illegal. I kept getting those rose-colored glasses knocked off. Although granted the divorce, not all disputes were resolved until three proceedings later. A judge told a friend in her messy court case, "You will not find the truth here." Fortunately for me, an acquaintance who has become a lifelong friend, shared a piece of the puzzle with me to help the truth reveal itself. I read Psalm 55 included in the morning prayer book on September 20, 2005. No coincidences, God does know.

I won a mug, which is still used occasionally today, from the Atlantic City Press for my submission of a 25 word or less entry for a contest. My children hid the package with the mug when it arrived in the mail, wrapped it, and gave it to me at Christmas. They appreciated the fact that my words were acknowledged. The challenge was to submit an editorial about saving money in a typical household.

Intact Families Cost Less, Atlantic City Press 12/7/2008:

The divorce rate is 50%. Two households, paramours and lawyers are expensive. If you're in an adulterous relationship, end it. Intact families cost less.

I have learned through my faith that everything does happen for a reason and that God reveals His plans incrementally. You think your life is mapped out perfectly, then life steps in. It is true we would not be able to handle the whole picture at one time. God makes clear the path we are to be on. When one advocates publicly, I learned that those who start out walking with us may drop back.

FAITH LIGHTS UP
THE DARKNESS

Peace of mind is often broken when we least expect it. The world will not give the peace that God gives. Achieving peace within oneself is not easy when in a storm. I always question when people tell me they were at peace with their decisions. I for one did not always feel peaceful or even good after many decisions. I got used to waiting for another shoe to drop. The negative reactions or voices of discontent were more numerous than those who patted me on the back or gave me credit. Besides names, my attitude was questioned. Damage to a reputation is difficult to repair, even when they know you intimately.

But when the waters are still, that may be when we have to be most alert. When all hell breaks loose, we just want to resume our normal routines and that feeling of being safe and peaceful. Peace in struggles comes through working with God. Prayer is the number one tool to create peace in your soul. The storm frightened the disciples in Mark 4:35-41 but who quieted it?

Saint Oscar Arnulfo Romero y Galdamez, called for an end to the violence in El Salvador. He was assassinated on March 24, 1980, at the altar, his place of work. He said, in reference to the violence in his nation,

It helps, now and then, to step back and take a long view. We may never see the end results, but that is the difference between the master builder and the worker. We are workers, not master builders, ministers, not messiahs. We are prophets of a future not our own.

In the mid-1990s, the parishes in my diocese implemented RENEW in which small groups gathered to read and discuss Scripture, apply it to real life, evangelize and participate in community life. I had been asked to deliver the invitation to join the groups at all Masses, and organized and led the telephone ministry. As a leader, I presented at our local conference. It is true, we do get prepared for the future. I was assigned the topic: The disciple is called to life in the community.

To accept the call to discipleship means to become involved in the formation of community ... we come to realize that love has everything to do with community, and communal actions help to rebuild the world ... Do we have a common vision and commitment to justice? ... How can we work through the conflict that arises whenever people gather to accomplish goals? It is to work through the hard times rather than run away, avoid, or pretend that none existed, or even say it should not be there. We must develop skills of communication. Speaking up for what we believe is risky, but the Gospel calls us to live a risky life. The principle of justice must be integrated into today's community life as it was in the early Christian community.

RENEW International https://www.renewintl.org/ headquarters is located in Plainfield, NJ, the town in which I grew up.

Managing our expectations in community life and balancing our faith with the real-world can create conflict; but it can also create connections. An eighth grader assumed he was challenging me because he said he wanted to write about Jesus. I told him to go ahead, but with any historical or spiritual leader, the essay parameters still had to be followed. I let a young second grader read a favorite story from the Bible at sharing time. He received the book as a gift. No one evangelized. Another child practiced her Hebrew prayer with us on a regular basis. She was nervous to recite it at her Hebrew class, but no one complained.

I discussed my work situation at length with Father Joe N. I asked him if I should continue to be a lector when the article came out about my experience with the district administration. He said the article was complimentary although I did not feel any emotion of joy. I wanted spiritual guidance to stay positive and on message when I addressed the parents. I shared that I thought what I had to say would hurt people. He reassured me that the truth does hurt, but it is for the best.

Scheduled to meet with him after Mass, I had chills when he began his homily with a reference to the Holocaust since my prepared speech also referenced the mandated school curriculum. Father Joe N. was a firm believer in bringing the world into focus when writing his homilies. He often quoted the belief that, when a priest prepares his homily, he should hold the newspaper in one hand and the Bible in the other. I held both for my speech. That philosophy was not unique to Father Joe; other noted theologians subscribed to it. It makes perfect sense. God sees the bigger picture. The Bible is about salvation history. Most authors will identify a source of inspiration. The Bible is inspiring. I write with Scripture and the news in mind.

On May 19, 1998, the Psalm at Mass was Psalm 138. "In the presence of angels, I will sing your praises" is the response to this psalm. On that day, I turned around to see that the Jesus statue's right hand extended out. His right hand did guide me. Motivated to buy flowers for one kindergarten teacher, I found an angel statue cradling a cat to give to my replacement. The new teacher needed prayer and to see that I did not hold her accountable.

On the Friday night after the address on May 18, my daughter, her friend, and I ordered take-out at the Chinese restaurant. We sat and waited as the chefs were preparing our meals. A woman and a man were sitting next to us, so we exchanged pleasantries. The woman, who said she was a nurse, spoke so calmly and profoundly. I admired her soft voice and told her so, since I was worried, and I do not always speak with such calmness. The woman told me "Gardening is good for the soul." I took it as a message. I like to exchange names with people with whom I have faith conversations, and this time was no different. The woman told me her name was Mary, and then introduced her husband as Joseph. God is not subtle. With their names and our names, all pointing to Mary, Jesus was in our midst. Since my mother and father were dead, Jesus sent reassuring parental role models.

The next morning, two mothers knocked at my back door with a plant. One was an aunt of my daughter's friend who was still visiting, and the other was the mother who challenged the three strikes rule. They specifically told me the plant was meant to be planted. God confirmed His sense of humor a second time to me, as I do not have a green thumb. Nevertheless, I planted them as instructed. "Gardening is good for the soul" confirmed in real time that day. I am thankful I had witnesses to the connections.

With the message, a spiritual one, I also did weeding. There were areas in my life that did not live up to the Christian teaching. Matthew 7:5, "Take the log out of your own eye before you pluck the splinter from someone else's" did not go unnoticed by me. I was harder on myself after April 22 than anyone else. Scandals hurt. I dove into Scripture more and more.

Scripture and prayer became my comfort zone. I was in a battle. I recited the St. Michael prayer for defense and read the Scripture about Moses. As long as Moses kept his hands raised in prayer, his people were winning the battle. When his hands were lowered, the enemy would win (Exodus 17). A rock to sit on and friends to hold up his arms kept them raised. My church friends were prayerful, welcoming and probably more aware than I thought. They did raise me up in prayer. Psalm 91 is meant for those in battle also.

In my search for answers in 1998, I came upon a card with the Serenity Prayer: "God grant me the courage to change the things I can change, the serenity to accept those I cannot change, and the wisdom to know the difference. But God grant me the courage not to give up on what is right, even though it is hopeless." I purchased many of these prayer cards and gave them away. I was right but staying employed ... hopeless.

I started attending daily Mass regularly at the local Chapel. The Mass was at a good time, and I just wanted to hide. Father Peter had different ideas. When I explained to him the circumstances of my new free time, he said "One day in heaven you will get a tap on the shoulder with a thank you." His words were comforting, and we spoke often. He asked me to do the reading at Mass one day, and he continued to ask me. He would not let me hide.

Father Larry, a wise, kind, elderly priest, lived at the Missionaries of the Sacred Hearts. At the age of fifty-eight, he started a side career. He became a sculptor. His artwork, depicting people of faith, is still displayed around the world, including right in front of my parish church. He celebrated Mass regularly. One day his message was about rejection. He looked right at me when he said, "You have been rejected." You are never too old to begin again.

The Pledge of Allegiance resonated in my heart all year long for my Courageous Cats. I loudly pledged, "Liberty and Justice, for all!" each morning. Clearly, when we suffer injustices, no matter how slight, we must work harder to right them for ourselves so as to benefit others. Suffering is a part of our earthly life, but God is one of justice and mercy. As the class and I recited the Pledge of Allegiance, injustices needed to be righted.

No one with their eyes open could have gone untouched by the shootings that year. Sadly, we could accept gang violence, violence in families. But children killing children proved to be a different story. People were reactive, not proactive.

JUSTICE: God's Forgotten Attribute written by Anthony Seton in The Catholic Answer[20] found its way into my hands. "However, in our joy at this unprecedented display of God's love, we ought not to lose sight of the other aspect of that love: His justice."

I wanted justice for all of us. The disruption changed our lives. Forgive, forget and move on did not work for me. Forgiveness does not need forgetting. I will never forget, and that is OK.

One day in the fall, my mother-in-law made a surprise week-day visit, rare for her. Her work schedule and ours meant we visited on weekends. She prayed for me in her daily Rosary, which includes reciting the "Our Father." God inspired her to be a friend the same day a white box truck pulled into my driveway unex-pectedly. The men knocked at my back door. They apologized but told me the Superintendent instructed them to deliver my school supplies. I had ignored correspondence advising me to pick them up. I did not want the supplies. I had left them to be used, but the Superintendent had the materials packed up. The maintenance men asked me where I wanted the boxes placed. I looked at the small shed and I told them to put the boxes on the street. I sorted through a few for supplies to give to a new teacher. Then I put a big sign saying "Free, I have no use for these anymore." A few people stopped. Free is good.

I was at my children's school the next week with the commu-nity recreation director. A man walked in with the decorative flags, explaining how he got them. Glances exchanged. The supplies that were not taken made it to the garbage trucks. I did not miss the items even two weeks later. If I had ever returned to classroom teaching, I would have purchased all new supplies.

Father Wags and Father Brad contributed spiritually, although not formally. Father Wags' homily about the hammer and the nail rang true: the nail that sticks up must be hammered down. Father Brad often mentioned his family and life experiences with siblings since he had a large family. Not in the mood one Sunday to hear anything about his life, God humbled my attitude as Father Brad spoke of his murdered friend.

Even in a workshop which I led at a juvenile detention center, the class recognized Jesus. I wore my pin and got compliments from the detained youth. We talked about making lemonade. Their counselor opened up his lapel to show me his St. Paul pin. He admired my courage to wear the Sacred Heart pin on the outside of my blazer.

The story, with differing versions from *The Star Thrower*[21], tells of a little boy who walked along a beach picking up starfish and throwing them back into the ocean. A man comes up to him, asking what and why are you doing this? Looking at the numbers on the beach, the man questioned the efforts. The little boy tells the man that his effort has made a difference to this one and continued with his one-on-one rescue.

Children are like starfish; sometimes they get washed into situations that are beyond their capabilities, comfort zones, or optimal learning/living environments. Anyone living on the spectrum of life can say the same.

According to a description on a website for Ocean Jewelry, https://oceanjewelrystore.com/starfish-symbolism-spiritual-meanings-powers/ "a starfish represents an ability to renew oneself. The starfish spirit animal represents heightened senses and sensory feelings. It encourages you to trust your instincts and listen to your inner voice." Starfish can regenerate but they must live in salt water.

Have you ever rescued a starfish? Have you ever stopped to turn a bug over so it can continue on its way? How do you survive when out of your comfort zone, you get tossed around or pulled suddenly from your natural habitat? To whom do you turn for help and strength?

I turned to the One who calmed the storm.

HOPE FOR THE FUTURE

Ask God for wisdom in connecting the dots and completing the puzzles in your life. Use your intuition: it is your gift of fear because we do get glimpses. When is a coincidence, not one?

We cannot prevent anything without a connection. Violence, broken laws, lies, retaliation, and evil impact us all. Take notice of dates, anniversaries and holy days (regardless of religion) which can trigger evil into action. People who commit violent acts often expose their plans before executing them.

It is a big country but a small world. In a Walt Disney World, Orlando, Florida hotel laundry room, I met a counselor from Jonesboro. We chatted for three hours, folding laundry together as my family played in the pool. It had been several years after the shooting. I told her how the actions of Shannon Wright had impacted me. She told me Jonesboro was like a war zone that day. Other schools were involved but did not suffer as the middle school did. Shannon Wright's husband had since remarried. In an interview on the twentieth anniversary, her son said he became a teacher. "After her death, I told my friends I would never let her name be forgotten, at least in my circles."

The Current, March 5, 2008: God Makes Heroes of Ordinary People

It seems that in the Old Testament, the people chosen by God to be leaders and or role models seem to perform extraordinary feats through the power of God. Noah built an ark. Moses brought down plagues, parted waters and led millions of people across the desert. David slew a giant, and Daniel stayed in the lion's den.

In the New Testament, Jesus and the people of faith demonstrated the power of God through ordinary means. Jesus used water and turned it into wine (John 2:1-11). He told stories and the people of faith listened. He healed with the words, "Take your mat, get up, and walk" (John 5:8). He used spit and mud to cure a blind man. He broke bread and drank wine. And He dined with common criminals.

The true role models of today are people, who through ordinary eloquence demonstrate the power of God. Rosa Parks sat on a bus; Martin Luther King preached and walked … firemen use trucks and hoses, and a mother, trying to save her baby, stays bedridden for months.

Shannon Wright, an ordinary teacher, took a few steps … It happened ten years ago this March 24. Her few steps took her life but saved the life of another. Indeed, "Only with difficulty does one die for a just person, though perhaps for a good person one might even find the courage to die" (Romans 3:7). Find hope in the ordinary. You never know when it is the power of God at work.

The love of children, well behaved or a hot mess, changes our hearts to do what we must to protect them. What would you do if a child in your class risked injury to self and others?

Would you accept the risks of seeking assistance? Would you allow a tragedy under your watch? Would you speak up or shut down? Those are questions to answer in a violent world. Many have answered with their lives. Do you have hope for the future, enough to speak up out of your comfort zone? A person without hope remains silent.

Volumes have been written on the who, what, when where and why of tragedies. An industry of professional trainers or security experts teaches or coordinates drills, while police train for rescue and recovery. Journalists living near or covering the shootings and professors at injured schools write. Survivors have forums. Bloodshed draws a crowd with flowers. Cottage industries grow with each failure.

At one point, when I was leading a few workshops, I thought I would join the cottage industry on prevention, but my family remained my first priority. I did lead some workshops through a statewide educational training center.

I distributed the *Guide To Safe Schools* to every teacher who would take one. At one workshop a few teachers were annoyed. I explained that guiding students involves safety. The district which had those annoyed teachers had a reality in view moment just one week later when a kid on a bus attacked others with a knife. Confused as those teachers may have been, they must have realized safety is for all staff.

In an inner-city high school, the staff had a welcoming attitude to a workshop. I used a poster of *The Scream* by Edvard Munch, 1893. Does it remind you of another iconic gesture caught on film in a movie about a child left at home? Do you scream every time you hear, "We did not think it could happen here." You are not alone. One teacher, wearing a tie with the Scream image, appreciated everything I handed out. Maybe he had felt like screaming too.

I tried this penny activity in a few workshops. Take a full penny roll and crack it open, hit it hard so the pennies scatter on the table. Now take a new roll and put the coins in it. How do you approach the task, one penny at a time? Do you pick up several or do you take a swipe and hope they all get in on the first try? Is the task so tedious that you still have that huge jar of pennies and no rolls with which to do this? Would you rather use a machine to count your pennies? Do you not have pennies because we swipe credit cards instead? I have no scientific documentation, but with the different techniques, the one-on-one aides took one penny at a time. In life, many try the swipe method and leave "pennies" behind.

How do you tackle completing a puzzle? Do you have a plan? Do you find all the end pieces first? Do you keep the greater picture in mind? Do you buy the puzzles that do not show you the picture?

I started writing this years ago and even floated this in a very bare bones format to publishers. I did not save the letter, but one responded with not being interested in the "trials and tribulations of a teacher"—his words, not mine. His company published the story of the mother of Columbine killer, Dylan Klebold. No one minded selling the trials and tribulations of the mother of a deranged young man. I did listen to an interview years ago to try to comprehend her story. Why did she write? Did she want to warn people? She must still have hope.

My family did go through a lot of stress through my ordeal. At the start we faced financial instability and dealing with the loss of my reputation. In 2005, the divorce, in which my advocacy in 1998 was used against me, challenged every aspect of our normal life. Was my decision to ask for a workshop too much? Is the messenger to blame? Did I get what I deserved?

Hope comes into play when we get back up after every knockdown.

I saw a social media post a few years ago, where the student described a much happier path as an adult. What people mean for evil, God can use for good.

I continue to have hope for the future. I am a refugee from public education, but still root for it. Despite its many flaws, is the alternative an uneducated population? Not everyone can home teach or pay for private education, neither of which are sanctuaries of truth. I have a greater respect for schools that do not accept federal funds. They have hope! With a jog of the memory from 1970s association mugs, "Nobody ever said teaching would be easy." Let us hope every person who enters a classroom understands that timeless message.

In the child's book, *Pete the Cat, I Love My White Shoes*,[22] the cat gets his shoes dirty, but he keeps his cool. Like the "get there the best way you know how" words from my past, "no matter what you step in, keep walking along and singing your song." This is a new edition to my repertoire of favorites. If you do not get some dirt kicked up on you in life, you are not living your true life.

The poet and teacher, Elizabeth Lee Bates, composed *America the Beautiful* in 1893 as she made the journey up Pikes Peak, the original name for the poem. She took a journey, saw a view from a mountaintop, and memorialized it for the future. She expressed hope. Whether the mountain is physical in nature or a metaphor for life, the climb teaches us along the way; and so we write.

The molehill made into a mountain on April 20, 1998, did change my life and I am thankful that I found inner strength. Climbing strengthened my heart muscle and voice.

The Current December 16, 2010: There Is Liberty in Law
Two things that make America great are law and order. Those are not only my thoughts, but they are also the words of many immigrants I worked with for five years in an ESL program. The poet wrote in *America the Beautiful* of liberty in law, just not so many laws that our spirits are broken and not so many lawbreakers that our liberty is threatened.

> O beautiful for spacious skies,
> For amber waves of grain,
> For purple mountain majesties
> Above the fruited plain!
> America! America!
> God shed His grace on thee
> And crown thy good with brotherhood
> From sea to shining sea!
>
> O beautiful for pilgrim feet,
> Whose stern, impassioned stress
> A thoroughfare for freedom beat
> Across the wilderness!
> America! America!
> God mend thine every flaw,
> Confirm thy soul in self-control,
> Thy liberty in law!

O beautiful for heroes proved
In liberating strife,
Who more than self their country loved
And mercy more than life!
America! America!
May God thy gold refine,
Till all success be nobleness,
And every gain divine!

O beautiful for patriot dream
That sees beyond the years
Thine alabaster cities gleam
Undimmed by human tears!
America! America!
God shed His grace on thee
And crown thy good with brotherhood
From sea to shining sea!

There is still beauty to be found in our many flaws if we recognize them and do better.

I submitted the following essay written in the summer of 1997 for publication, but it did not make the cut. However, I saved it, and looking through the rear-view mirror, the reflection has a prophetic tone. I had hope for the future.

From the Teacher's Desk- One Teacher's Perspective Summer 1997

Summertime and the living is easy, but not far from my mind is the start of another school year. The calendar reads late July, so it is time to put on my thinking cap. Preliminary lesson plans, scheduling and room revamping what will be part of the August ritual. After this recess I am able to review and revitalize activities for the year to come! It is with renewed energy that I prepare in earnest to greet, care for, and work with the children and families who will become mine for the 1997-98 academic year.

My restful days have been spent reclining and reading novels, newspapers, suspense suicides and reminders of the educational system from which I draw my summer reserve. Report card ratings as well as editorials and reports inform me about the status of the educational system. Critiques capture my attention. Family and friends share their opinions.

My view from the teacher's desk says the educational system has been managing the herculean task of providing many opportunities for those in search of learning. Daily, the system must work for and with the multiple personalities of America. American schools do not just educate. They socialize, cancel, recreate, rehabilitate, renovate, and report.

Education is generally not about books or buildings: it's about people. Dealing with people always involves walking a fine line. When the line is crossed, people respond. Emotional bonds are such that the reactions are rarely neutral.

The politics of the day cloud educational decisions and outcomes. Movement is difficult when groups are polarized. Special interest groups continue to lobby for public education to subsidize private education. Funding sources and budgets are continuously debated and often defeated. Local governing bodies work against their local school districts. Business is booming for companies who take advantage of school business cuts. They have learned to boost their sales through PTA or PTO solicitations. Education foundations are noble in concept, but hours are taken from administrators to discuss fund raisers.

School boards will question the intentions of personnel in contract negotiations, but if one were to write job descriptions of those teaching today, it would be surprising to see a list of job responsibilities. From support positions to school Superintendent, no one wears just one hat. The diversity and variety, associated with traditional routines, are attractive features of this career. Continuing education for all staff members is the norm, not the exception. Workshops, seminars, coursework, and individual enrichment or opportunities are provided for and sought after by employees. Expenses are often paid directly out of pocket.

Professionalism is paramount. The professional attitude of employees must be considered when the bottom line of economics is at play. Renderings are made by some who have no direct comprehension of what it means to work in the educational system. Strong determination of district staff continues the educational process even when interference from outside management arises.

Responsibilities should be shared. Assuming that the teacher is solely accountable for the learning taking place is foolish and selfish. That attitude underestimates the pupil's ability, in addition to undermining the importance of good and involved parenting. Having realistic, positive discussions with children about their responsibilities in learning and the parts others play will help them prepare for their roles in life. Empowering children to take responsibility allows them to experience pride and satisfaction. Exhibiting faith in the teachers facilitates the child's developing sense of confidence. Challenging the educational staff to account is empowering.

It is on this note that a thank you is extended to the parents and children with whom I have worked. Understanding the importance of support, trust, and follow through, the parents asked questions, became involved, and did not question the professional motivations behind my choices. The children demonstrated by asking questions, their involvement and decision making. Becoming better students helps make me a better teacher.

So, as I read the last chapter and recycle back-to-school ads, I return to my desk where the view is radiant. There will be revelry and rejoicing because, regardless of reproachful rhetoric, American public education is rewarding. I will receive a rich return on my investment because of the resourcefulness of the people for whom I root.

How does it apply to education in 2024? How can this generation make the educational system better for all? Are you willing to go stand at the microphone or write a few editorials? Do you have hope for the future of public education today?

Here are few truths I have learned.

You do not need a classroom to teach ... The risk is worth it ... The answers come from listening to God ... "We are His hands eyes, feet and mouths here on earth" - Saint Teresa of Avila ... I am neither a priest, nor a rabbi ... Not everyone believes ... I will always remember Shannon Wright and Ping ... The seeds you plant matter ... Children are watching and listening to everything we do and say ... some broken relationships do heal.

ACKNOWLEDGMENTS

Anna and Chris
A Beautiful Butterfly and her mom
Carlino's Courageous Cats and their parents
Children who have fallen through the cracks
Parents who brought me the plant and wrote letters in support
To those in education who have given their lives for the children
under their care

END NOTES

1. (De Becker 1997)
2. (Casey at Bat n.d.)
3. (The Empty Pot n.d.)
4. (McCanna 1998)
5. (Parker 1998)
6. (Canfield, Chicken Soup for the Soul 1993)
7. (Cat1)
8. (The Perfect Assist n.d.)
9. (Covey n.d.)
10. (Canfield 1993)
11. (Volaykova 1994)
12. (Archer 2019)
13. (Stenard 2019)
14. (Kass 2014)
15. (Kraybill, Nott and Weaver-Zecher 2007)
16. (Roy 2009)
17. (Spirituals Triumphant, Old and New in 1927. 1927)
18. (De Becker, The Gift of Fear n.d.)
19. (Olweus 1993)
20. (Seton n.d.)
21. (Eiseley 1969)
22. (Dean 2010)

Milton Keynes UK
Ingram Content Group UK Ltd.
UKHW040900180424
441312UK00002B/43